FRAGONARD

FRAGONARD

JACQUES THUILLIER

Professor at the Collège de France, Paris

SKIRA

RIZZOLI
NEW YORK

First published 1967
Revised paperback edition 1987

Published in the United States of America in 1987 by

Rizzoli INTERNATIONAL PUBLICATIONS, INC.
597 Fifth Avenue/New York 10017

© 1987 by Editions d'Art Albert Skira S.A., Geneva

Translated from the French by Robert Allen

Printed in Switzerland

Library of Congress Cataloging-in-Publication Data

Thuillier, Jacques.
    Fragonard.

    Includes index.
    1. Fragonard, Jean Honoré, 1732-1806.
2. Painters—France—Biography.   3. Painting, French.
4. Painting, Modern—17th-18th centuries—France.
I. Title.
ND553.F7T413   1987   759.4   87-45552
ISBN 0-8478-0885-8 (Rizzoli: pbk.)

CONTENTS

I
FRAGONARD,
OR THE HAPPY PAINTER

The Triumph of Venus, undated. Oil sketch for a ceiling decoration.

A FAMOUS name, but a faceless one. When Rembrandt's name is mentioned, we see in our mind's eye that coarse, common face whose every line and crease the painter pored over from his adolescence to his death, thus making us no less familiar with his appearance than with his art. Fouquet's keen, restless eye, Van Dyck's sensuous elegance, the gravity of Poussin—behind every great work we can usually see, more or less clearly, the face of the man who did it. In the eighteenth century, though Chardin was discretion itself, his still lifes reflect the good soul's round face, and behind the elegant smiles of La Tour's models we can sense the pastelist's mask fluctuating between worldly nonchalance and the grin of lunacy. But who knows the face of Fragonard?

That is not for any lack of portraits. He left several by his own hand —rapid sketches in red or black chalk, long preserved by his family and therefore offering a certain guarantee of authenticity. But they date from his old age and most of them are too summary to reveal the man within. The attribution to Claude Hoin of a head and shoulders on gray paper, heightened with red and white chalk, is now generally accepted;

but the frozen, distant expression tells us nothing about the sitter himself. Five or six paintings also claim to be portraits of Fragonard. One is the oval in the Grasse Museum entitled *Portrait of a Young Painter*; though charming, it is hardly plausible. Another is the head viewed from three quarters (in a private collection) that has been thought to be a self-portrait of the painter in his youth. These pictures resemble each other so little that quite likely not all of them are apocryphal. An official of the Revolutionary government set down the following description of Fragonard at the age of sixty-two: "four feet eleven inches, high forehead, medium-sized nose, gray eyes, average mouth, round chin, marks of smallpox." But all this is not enough to give us the portrait truer than the truth of officialdom which posterity hopes will one day disclose the painter's real presence.

This point, though seemingly unimportant, must be investigated for it involves Fragonard's entire œuvre. We are apt, no doubt, to think that, being naturally amiable and even nonchalant, he was obsessed by the looking glass: his painting is not concerned with man's intimate secrets. Human destiny is not the subject of that brilliant work. This our romantic bent inclines us to regret. The last century—imitated in this readily by our own—endeavored to fill the gap and give Fragonard's life a touch of Casanova, a hint of Restif de La Bretonne. But we must accept the evidence: however much his work makes us hanker for a romantic story, all we have is the biography of an honest man.

Can Fragonard have been a great painter and nothing else?

"LE BON FRAGO"

"IF I wanted to paint a child's joy and gaiety, its whims, its caresses, its happiness, I would take him as my model. If I wanted to paint the qualities of friendship, its gentleness, kindness, solicitude, tenderness, I would again take him as my model. The most amiable of philosophers, the cleverest and most graceful of painters, the best of husbands, the most affectionate and constant of friends, the most attentive and solicitous of teachers." Or again: "A child whom a trifle vexes and a trifle pacifies: truly caprice's nurseling." There we have the spiritual portrait of Fragonard. A little flattering, perhaps, because it was written by a woman and we can recognize the blandishments of an affectionate sister-in-law for an old man. But other witnesses record the same traits. About a hundred years ago, the last descendant of the Bergerets, one of the families closest to Fragonard, still recalled that "the whole house was at his beck and call; young and old had accepted all his whims. They ate only dishes that pleased 'le bon Frago,' who did not fail to take advantage of the very real affection he inspired."

Fragonard, the spoilt child. Spoilt by his family circle and by a society that made much of him. Spoilt by a fortune that smiled upon him nearly all his life and even spared him the annoyance of glory. Let us examine his life in detail, yet quite briefly, eliminating all the superfluous ornament accumulated by successive authors; we shall find that it was all of a piece, and all happy.

Jean-Honoré Fragonard was born at Grasse, near Cannes, on April 5, 1732. His surname would seem to indicate a distant Italian origin; and in fact an ancestor of his, at the end of the sixteenth century, claimed to be a native of a suburb of Milan. There has been much dispute as to whether François Fragonard, the artist's father, was a rich merchant or simply a haberdasher's assistant. Be that as it may, there are documents to prove that the Fragonards had always been tradesmen in easy circumstances. François risked most of the fortune inherited from his father —at that time speculation was rife even in the remote provinces—in François-Nicolas Du Perier's fire pump venture. The project failed and he went to Paris to try to salvage part of his capital. It was not the sort of business that could be arranged in a few days and he ended up by settling there for good.

Young Fragonard must have been six years old at the time. The southern sun, the tall cypresses, the fountains, the bare-armed housewives gossiping as they dried their washing in the sun—all these visions of the sunny South must have slumbered as dazzling memories in the mind of the little Parisian he became. Italy awakened them one day.

His younger brother died at ten months. Now an only child and heir to his uncle Pierre, who had taken holy orders, he did not push his studies very far. When he was about thirteen, or perhaps even earlier—the date is not known—he was placed as a clerk with a notary. But the boy was obsessed with painting, and drawing was his favorite pastime. His parents noted the fact and took him to see Boucher, the most fashionable painter of the day. Those Parisian craftsmen and tradesmen, who were familiar with churches full of famous paintings and rubbed shoulders with rich and honored painters, had an eye for art and seldom thwarted a vocation. That is how a great many of the painters and sculptors who formed the backbone of French art under the old order were recruited.

Jeroboam Sacrificing to the Idols, 1752. Oil.

Boucher found the boy totally untrained and sent him over to Chardin. What a magnificent tradition it is that places Fragonard's first beginnings under such dual sponsorship! And apparently it is not a figment. Chardin treated him like an apprentice, as was the custom of the guild; he set him menial tasks and gave him prints to copy. Patience was not the young Provençal's strong point and Chardin finally decided he had no future and packed him off. Taking his courage in both hands, he called on Boucher again and showed him some sketches after pictures he had seen in the Paris churches. This time—it must have been about 1748—Boucher accepted him as a pupil and it was not long before he prized his talent so highly that he gave him his regard and friendship. That decided Fragonard's career.

In 1752 Boucher encouraged him, though not a pupil of the Academy, to enter the competition for the Grand Prix for painting, which opened the door to Rome. The young man's budding talent must have been already recognized, for his application was accepted. He used the official theme, *Jeroboam Sacrificing to the Idols*, to compose the winning picture, which is still kept at the Ecole des Beaux-Arts in Paris and shows considerable ability for a youth of twenty. Gabriel de Saint-Aubin, eight years his senior, was only awarded second prize and was so furious that he broke with the Academy and thereafter devoted himself entirely to his mania for drawing.

There was a rule that the young artists destined for Rome should first complete their training at the Ecole Royale des Elèves Protégés, which was located in a house in the courtyard of the old Louvre. Fragonard entered it in May 1753. At that time the head of the school was Carle van Loo, an excellent teacher. His wife, a former singer and daughter of the violinist Somis, still possessed the magnificent voice that had conquered Paris and she kept a motherly eye on the pupils. Fragonard must have been happy under their wing. When a place became free at the French Academy in Rome, in 1754, he and his fellow-students signed a petition asking to be "allowed to finish their term under such a good teacher." In addition to painting and engraving, the curriculum comprised history, mythology and geography. And every day Lépicié expounded Ovid, Homer, Herodotus, Livy and Dom Calmet. If the onetime errand-boy later proved capable of acting as scholarly companion to Saint-Non and guide to Bergeret, if the best circles took pleasure in his company and even accepted his amiable tyranny, it was thanks, no doubt, largely to that felicitous establishment.

But to Rome he went at last, in the autumn of 1756, accompanied by his fellow-students Monnet and the two Brenets, as well as by kindly Madame Van Loo, who took advantage of the expedition to visit her family in Turin. At that time the head of the French Academy in Rome was Natoire, a delicate, scholarly painter to whom our generation has not yet given his due, and a scrupulous director. We can trace the progress and hesitations of "Flagonard," as Natoire insisted on calling him, in a long series of reports addressed to the Surintendant des Bâtiments, the Marquis de Marigny, Madame de Pompadour's brother. The director was uneasy at first but in the end he too showed his pupil esteem and affection. It is hard to say which, in their correspondence, is more to be admired, whether Natoire's caution or the intelligent concern of Marigny, who showered the most signal favors on Fragonard. The latter found (and gave) such pleasure in Rome that he asked for (and was

The Gardens of the Villa d'Este, Tivoli ("The Little Park"), c. 1760. Oil.

Coresus Sacrifices Himself to Save Callirrhoe (first version), c. 1762-1765. Oil.

granted) a fourth year of study there and later board and lodging for a fifth. In the meantime he had gained the friendship of the Abbé de Saint-Non, whose guest and collaborator he was during the whole summer of 1760 in the Villa d'Este at Tivoli, famous for its beautiful gardens.

Claude-Richard de Saint-Non, onetime councillor-magistrate at the second Chambre des Enquêtes of the Paris Parliament, was thirty-two years old. He had recently been assured of a good income from the Abbey of Saint-Pierre at Pothières, near Châtillon-sur-Seine. His father was a receiver general of finance, and on his mother's side he was descended from the Boullongnes, a dynasty of famous painters culminating in a controller general of France. So it is no wonder that he combined a solid fortune with a decided taste for the arts, which he even dabbled in himself. With a passion for painting and music, eager to see and draw everything, he had come to Rome with the idea of laying up, as the Comte de Caylus said, "a store to keep him going for the rest of his life."

On his arrival in Rome with Taraval, Saint-Non at once became intimate with Hubert Robert and was soon on friendly terms with Fragonard. Young, gay, spontaneous, yet of even temper, the latter was the ideal companion. Saint-Non, who called Fragonard his "little comrade," showed him Naples and took him back with him to Paris in the spring of 1761, passing through Bologna, Florence, Venice, Verona, Parma and Genoa, visiting churches and viewing famous collections. In

Coresus Sacrifices Himself to Save Callirrhoe, exhibited at the Salon of 1765. Oil.

Coresus Sacrifices Himself to Save Callirrhoe (detail), Salon of 1765. Oil.

this way Fragonard acquired a thorough, first-hand knowledge of Italian painting. He also acquired a lifelong friend and patron.

One can never insist enough on the importance of the years Fragonard spent in Italy and the "grand tour" that crowned them. Rome and the Roman Campagna led the southerner he was to rediscover a strong link with reality, a direct feeling for nature, that protected him all his life against the illusions of intellectual speculation and worldly refinements. He did a great many drawings after the old masters; collected and engraved in aquatint by Saint-Non, they formed the nucleus of the quarto compilation entitled *Fragments choisis dans les Peintures et les Tableaux des Palais et des Eglises de l'Italie* (Fragments Selected from among the Paintings and Pictures in the Palaces and Churches of Italy) published from 1770 on. He also did several spirited etchings after Lanfranco, Ricci and Tiepolo, and the influence of those studies can be traced through his entire œuvre.

At twenty-nine Fragonard was no longer a student but a full-fledged painter. Natoire himself tells us that he had sent and brought back from Rome a "quantity of fine pieces." He was now on the immediate threshold of an official career, with admission to the Academy as a first step. He sought a subject for a picture and, after much hesitation, chose the pathetic finale of an opera that was popular at the time. He submitted his *Coresus Sacrificing Himself to Save Callirrhoe* to the Academy in March 1765 and was received as a member with, as Marigny himself said, "a unanimity and an enthusiasm of which there have been few examples." More important still, when the picture was shown at the Salon of that year it was highly acclaimed by the general public. "Little Saint-Non," as Caylus calls him, was a regular guest at Madame Geoffrin's Mondays; he was connected with enlightened financial circles, with Boulogne, Roslin, Watelet, Lalive de Jully, all great collectors who occasionally toyed with brush or burin and whose dearest ambition was to be admitted as an honorary counsellor or associate member of the Royal Academy. One could wish for no better patron. Moreover, Cochin, who was devoted to Fragonard, recommended him to Marigny and obtained for him the favor of a studio in the Louvre.

But after making such a splendid start, the painter abandoned the highway of official art. He did accept a few commissions: two overdoors for the Château de Bellevue, which belonged to the royal princesses, two pictures for the dining-room in the king's private apartments at Versailles, a set for a drawing-room at Louveciennes, Madame du Barry's favorite residence. But he was in no hurry either to solicit or to execute them and in the end not one of those works was ever set in place. He was quite satisfied with the patronage of such art lovers as the Marquis de Veri, La Reynière, Randon de Boisset, and Varanchan, who very soon got into the habit of paying fancy prices for his pictures.

It is worth while repeating, once again, a story Collé tells in his *Memoirs*, for it is symbolic of the painter's choice and may well have made a decisive impact on it. Doyen, shortly after gaining such marked success at the Salon with his *St Genevieve Putting an End to a Pestilence* now in the Church of Saint-Roch in Paris, was summoned by the Baron de Saint-Julien. That gentleman received him in his "little house," overwhelmed him with attentions and, indicating his mistress, said: "I should like you to paint Madame seated on a swing and being pushed by a bishop. Me you shall place in a position where I can observe the legs of that charming girl, and better still if you want to enliven your picture . . ." The point of the story is that Saint-Julien, who had even more wit than impudence, was receiver general of the French clergy. Coming from an enemy, his action would have been a nasty cut; but under the circumstances it had the neat touch of the libertine. Doyen was almost struck speechless by the proposition which his devout religious picture had prompted, and received the offer with ill grace. He merely mentioned Fragonard's name and took his leave. Boucher's former pupil did not believe that Jeroboam and Coresus could prevent him from limning a pretty pair of legs. The result was *The Swing*, now in the Wallace Collection, London. All Paris, having heard the story, doted over the pink and blue gem. What more was needed to make Fragonard all the rage?

The Swing dates from 1767. Until the Revolution the painter lived a life of tranquil ease, by-passed by honors but not by fame. He enjoyed a practically limitless freedom unmarred by social duties or material cares. If his work did not clash with the taste of his day, the reason is that it was in perfect harmony with that taste and perhaps even helped to form it. His rejection of an academic career is conclusive proof of this. Few artists have insisted more than Fragonard on preserving their freedom; few have been more entirely dedicated to their art.

Fragonard's life seems to have run its course between his studio in the Louvre and the few houses he frequented more as a friend and intimate than as a protégé. One of the rare events worth mentioning is a second

The Swing, 1767. Oil.

The Swing (detail), 1767. Oil.

trip to Italy with Bergeret de Grancourt, receiver general for the district of Montauban and treasurer of the Order of St Louis, who paid all expenses. Bergeret, who was related to Saint-Non because his first wife had been the Abbé's sister, was a man of taste and from the very start a great admirer of Fragonard. He was anxious to procure a guide capable of making him appreciate the beautiful things he was going to see. The expedition, which later took in Vienna, Prague, Dresden and Frankfurt, lasted from October 1773 to September 1774.

Four years earlier Fragonard, whose future was now assured, had married Marie-Anne Gérard, a girl from his home town. Her brother was living in Paris and she had come there to get commercial training. She was interested in miniature painting and apparently asked her compatriot to give her lessons. After her marriage, Madame Fragonard governed the household with a firm hand and till the end of her life shouldered all material cares. But she did not give up her painting. She had two children: a daughter, Rosalie, born in 1769, and a son, Alexandre-Evariste, born in 1780. Her younger sister, Marguerite, came from Grasse to join the family in 1775. She was only fourteen and could barely read and write. But she too became a pupil of Fragonard's, studied drawing and engraving, and soon made a name for herself.

The Revolution, which forced Doyen to flee as far afield as Russia and almost cost Hubert Robert his head, was kind to Fragonard. In France, artists—even those most loaded with honors—have always worshipped new ideas and bearded the authorities. Fragonard, no exception to the rule, became a freemason. In 1778, the man who had painted the *Girl Dancing Her Dog on Her Bed* composed in honor of Benjamin Franklin a pompous allegory after which Marguerite Gérard did the engraving that was her first masterpiece. He seems to have welcomed the Revolution. Madame Fragonard and Marguerite were among the twenty artists' wives who, in September 1789, went to the National Assembly with the jewelry they were sacrificing in order to wipe out the public debt, and whose patriotism was lauded in the Gazette. Incidentally, Saint-Non was so overcome by enthusiasm that he gave up half the income he received from his abbey. (He did not have to wait long before seeing—with rather less enthusiasm—the other half confiscated.)

As a matter of fact, Fragonard escaped some of the trouble in Paris. Rosalie's death in October 1788, shortly before her nineteenth birthday, was certainly the hardest blow the painter ever suffered. He was so deeply affected, we are told, that his health was undermined. The doctors advised a stay at Grasse. So early in 1790 Fragonard, his wife and Marguerite left Paris and stayed some time in the South with their cousins the Mauberts. It was not until a year later, in spring 1791, that they returned to Paris.

What a change they found! The affluent society that had made much of Fragonard and paid big prices for his pictures had scattered. Saint-Non died, penniless, at the end of the autumn. Interest on annuities was cut and cut again, and Fragonard's income dwindled. Luckily for him, David was a power in the world of art. He had, it seems, been helped by Fragonard, who was sixteen years his senior, at the beginning of his career; they had become close friends and, however paradoxical it may appear to us, in view of their very different styles and outlooks, they regarded each other with mutual esteem. Through the painter of *The Horatii*, the painter of *The Swing* obtained an appointment to the arts commission. This is what David wrote of Fragonard to press his claim: "Both a connoisseur and a great painter, he will devote his old age to the preservation of the masterpieces whose number he helped to increase in his youth." Opinions of David's fine revolutionary style may differ, but it would be wrong to view his words as an expression of haughty conde-scension. Fragonard was one of the most active members of the expert commission set up in the 1790s to organize what later became the Louvre Museum. The work, which seems to have taken up much of his time, continued until 1800.

At seventy, Fragonard still had a lively manner and a youthful heart. "Rotund, chubby, dapper, always lively, always gay, he had nice red cheeks, twinkling eyes, ruffled gray hair, and one could see him in the [Louvre] Galleries always dressed in a greatcoat or roquelaure of mixed gray cloth with neither hooks, frogs nor buttons, which the old fellow tied around his waist, when he was at work, with anything that came to hand—a rag or a bit of string. Everybody liked him." It is true that the glory of "little papa Fragonard" was at a low ebb, and the painter of *Coresus* did not enjoy the fervid admiration that surrounds some artists in their old age. But he took pleasure in the success of his sister-in-law and his son, who had become a pupil of David, and seems not to have been embittered.

We often hear the story told by the Goncourts that one hot day, on his way home from an errand in the Champ-de-Mars, Fragonard went into a café, ate an ice and was struck down by congestion of the brain. Gault de Saint-Germain, his contemporary and a good witness, merely says that he had "an illness that lasted a fortnight and whose only symptom was a long-drawn somnolence, at the end of which he passed away without pain or agony." His death certificate is dated August 22, 1806.

His son Alexandre-Evariste Fragonard was also a famous painter. It is the fashion nowadays to scorn his talent, which is either overlooked or judged by two or three official commissions. But a work like *The First Athenian Parricide*, engraved by Godefroy, though a little pompous, reveals the best qualities of the school of David. He was no less capable as a painter of landscapes than of large decorative works. His son Théophile became a painter too. He showed ability in book illustration and between 1835 and 1840 was scarcely less sought after by publishers than Gavarni or Tony Johannot. In 1847 Théophile Fragonard took a job with the Sèvres porcelain works where he came under the spell of the models left by Watteau, Boucher and his own grandfather, and even recaptured something of their spirit. He left a great many drawings and watercolors that show considerable facility and taste. He is one of the best exponents of the Pompadour style so dear to the Second Empire, and there is reason to believe that more than one of his works has been surreptitiously labeled with a more highly valued Christian name. His posterity lives on and today the name of Fragonard is still borne with distinction.

The Letter or Memories, undated. Oil.

FRAGONARD AND VIRTUE

I N a life that holds no surprises, one would like to find at least the spice of amorous adventures. Fragonard's art is entirely dedicated to woman. Could one imagine that his life was not so too?

> Hasten to paint all the fair ladies' charms,
> You'll be paid for your work in your models' arms.

That was the advice Boufflers received from the Chevalier de Bonnard. Fragonard's biographers had the same idea and tell us a delightful tale. At nineteen, all fire, gaiety and passion—after all it was the century of Cherubino—he was in love with Madame Boucher, then at the peak of her famous blonde beauty. Later, kind Madame Van Loo watched with motherly care over the favored pupil. In Rome the black-eyed women of Trastevere were quick to upset the boarders at the Academy, and the Abbé de Saint-Non was certainly not one to lecture against affairs in Naples or Venice. Back in Paris, we find Fragonard recognized as a great painter. All boudoir doors were open to him, including those of a trio of fashionable beauties known as the Dove sisters, and of Mademoiselle Guimard, a famous dancer with a fickle heart.

The Schoolmistress ("Now Say Please"), undated. Oil.

But the painter preferred marriage. This saddens his biographers, who join in depicting his spouse as a kind of shrew, a second Madame Diderot, a Madame Greuze without the charms of Gabrielle Babuti. The only quality they grant her is the possession of a young sister who lacked none of the gifts and graces and became Fragonard's disciple. Tender lessons, sweet secrets—this last transparent mystery is the close of the most sentimental of love stories.

In fact, a story is exactly what it was. For the whole thing was invented, or almost.

Far be it from me to claim that before his marriage Frago, an agreeable fellow and merry companion who pleased all those who came into contact with him, obeyed the strict laws of a virtue that was paid little honor in his day. The director of the French Academy in Rome sometimes had trouble over his boarders' love affairs, and in Paris every artist and writer has his mistress, be she abigail or marquise—and often both at once. But Fragonard has not taken us into his confidence and the worst tongues of his day are mute on this point. We must conclude that his love affairs were either very discreet or not too highly spiced.

As a matter of fact, all these legends, which are repeated by every author and so end up by receiving absolute credit, lack the slightest proof. Much importance is attached to a set of canvases on which girls are playing with doves—slightly veiled allusions, we are told, to three sisters who were better known for their charm than for their virtue. They were Marie-Catherine, Marie-Thérèse and Marie-Madeleine Riggieri, members of the Italian comedy troupe who were familiarly known as Mesdemoiselles Colombe. But the birds sacred to Venus are far more numerous in Greuze's pictures and Chénier's poems, and the alleged portraits show nothing more than the pretty, impersonal face, tip-tilted nose, large eyes and rosy complexion long favored by Fragonard. Two *tondi* discovered long ago in a house that once was theirs, and believed without proof to be their portraits, are a very slender foundation on which to build a love affair.

For Mademoiselle Guimard Fragonard certainly worked before quarreling with her. We have the story from Grimm himself, who tells how the painter took his revenge. What a fine pretext for conjuring up the storms of passion and calling every picture of a rather skinny woman a portrait of the dancer. Things have gone pretty far in this direction. How satisfying for a collector, how profitable for a dealer, to be able to join in a single picture two such famous names and a record of that unique bond between painting and dancing! But unfortunately Mademoiselle Guimard already had several acknowledged lovers and Grimm, who was not one to miss a piquant allusion, seems never to have dreamt of adding Fragonard's name to the list. What is more, the painter had not long been married at the time.

In fact, once he had gained success and affluence, Fragonard, like any other worthy middleclass citizen, married a woman from his home town. The marriage was certainly decided, if not arranged, by the two families, which, as is proved by documentary evidence, were on friendly terms at least since the painter's childhood. What an idea, to marry Marie-Anne Gérard, the daughter of a perfumer, with a heavy Provençal accent and barely five feet tall! It was, we are told, because poor Frago had to make amends for an accident: little Rosalie was born less than six months after the wedding. But our informants have forgotten to consult the documents, which prove that the contract was signed and her parents' consent obtained over a year before. They have asserted that

Portrait of the Artist's Wife Marie-Anne Fragonard, undated.
Brush and bistre wash on white paper.

The Cradle or The Happy Family, undated. Oil.

Marie-Anne was plain and disagreeable and have even given her a shade of a moustache. But the wash drawing preserved in the Besançon Museum—undoubtedly authentic because bequeathed by the architect Pâris, who knew Madame Fragonard very well—shows us nothing of the sort. The rather short nose, square chin, thick brows above dark eyes, and large mouth are typical of a not unattractive girl from the South. We can take it for granted that if Bergeret took Madame Fragonard with him to Italy and seated her opposite him in his coach, she was not a plain Jane. And if David, like a good neighbor, took care not to forget affectionate regards to Madame Fragonard at the close of a letter to Evariste, we may presume that the miniaturist was a worthy woman,

Head of a Young Man, undated. Oil.

and even something more. Besides, if Fragonard married that slip of a girl of twenty-three when he was close on forty, why should we believe that he had resigned himself to a marriage of convenience? After all, he was in such a hurry to consummate it that he did not wait for the wedding ceremony! And it was certainly not by mere chance, or to suit the taste of the day, that his brush inclined still more than before towards the motif of the young mother and her happy family.

In 1775 Marie-Anne's younger sister Marguerite joined the family. She seems to have soon developed, from an awkward, plain, provincial girl, into an elegant Parisienne and "when it became the fashion for women to leave their hair unpowdered, the style of her beauty created a sensation at the theater." As tall as her sister but with finer features, speaking with the same accent but with a certain grace, ignorant but aware of the fact, Marguerite Gérard bewitched everyone by her charming manners. A deep affection sprang up between master and pupil: all eye-witnesses agree in saying that the ageing painter adored his sister-in-law. Nor do they seem to imply anything more than they say.

"An innocent alliance of tastes and sympathies," is how the Goncourts define the relationship. But their successors have not shown the same discretion. A quantity of little notes written on blue paper in a childish hand and with a child's spelling were found among the family papers—tender little messages from Marguerite to the painter—and fell into his biographers' clutches. What better proof of his last love? How easy to imagine the famous *Music Lesson* transformed into a painting lesson! But they should have checked the dates. Those notes were written about the Year X (i.e. 1802-1803). Fragonard was a little old man of seventy, lively, domineering, penniless, and Marguerite a spinster of forty, still charming but hardly unsophisticated. It was she who now won the laurels, had a little money salted away, and indulged her "good friend," her "dear little papa," with flattery, dainties and even an occasional coin.

"When my good friend," she writes, "tells me he could find no pleasure anywhere if I wasn't by his side, my heart is so delighted that I would like never to leave him, even for a second, and to become his shadow in order to make him happy. Were I to say, my friend, that the wish to please him and the wish to work cause me in turn intense distress, that it costs me much to resist his desires..." What a confession! But let us read more carefully: what the old man wants is to have his sister-in-law there to amuse him, while she instead wants to work in the seclusion of her studio. Words of praise, little lectures, comparisons of love and friendship, marks of affection—what were they but the intimate exchanges that did not disdain an exalted style, the tokens of friendship so greatly favored in an age that delighted in Werther. Fragonard, instead, seems to have employed a more jocular tone. The good soul basked without scruple in the dual affection of Marie-Anne and Marguerite. "In his homely language," a witness says, "he used to call the two sisters his wenches."

If we need further evidence, David will serve our purpose once again. In a letter to the Minister Roland dated October 24, 1792, which the biographers take care not to quote, David mentions Fragonard as the example of "merit that hides itself" and ought to be rewarded by a "virtuous minister." He goes on to say that the painter "is well known for his talents, but what people do not know is his way of life and that of his honorable family; I recently described it to you, comparing it with the simple, patriarchal habits of our distant ancestors."

Not very satisfying for those of us who hanker after romance! How irritating to see Fragonard's life draw to a close after the manner of one of those pictures by Greuze that are appreciated so little nowadays! We should like the artist to resemble his work and his work to resemble the period, or rather the superficial idea of the period we too often insist upon. For on this point we do not hesitate to speak in the same breath of Fragonard and Boucher, though they belong to two generations that are worlds apart. Boucher was born in 1703; his pupil thirty years later. Fragonard belonged to an in-between generation that on one side bordered on the licentious, pleasure-loving society set up by the Regency, while inclining on the other to the middleclass sentiments, morality and happiness. All through history we find periods when the conquest of freedom, in both thought and morals, is sufficient justification for writers and painters alike; there are others, instead, when discipline prevails and the artist wants a house of his own and a good reputation among his neighbors. Art is the great adventure, the real passion. Rid of its romantic trappings, this simple, sober, pleasant way of life leads us to see Fragonard's work in a new light.

CAREER AND CHRONOLOGY

F RAGONARD, as far as we know, was anything but a vulgar dauber. Nor does the excellent Jules Renouvier seem to have been particularly partial to coarse language. Yet, in his *Histoire de l'Art pendant la Révolution*, we find this phrase: "A painter in every fiber of his being, he felt so possessed by the demon of that art that he was wont to say, in words that must be left unaltered because they are his very own: 'I would paint with my backside'."

Now we know the whole story. Let us leave aside the man and forget his presumed love affairs. In the last analysis, what really counts in Fragonard is always the artist.

If we could only follow him in every stage of his development, in every detail of his career. Unfortunately, there is no chronological record of his work. His first biographers, the Goncourts and Portalis, made no effort to establish it with any accuracy. A recent study deserves credit for making a more serious endeavor to do so. But there are many points where the dates are still vague, arbitrary, even contradictory. Should his pictures be subdivided according to their subject matter into narrow periods, as if he was Picasso or Dubuffet? Should the gaps be filled by inserting isolated canvases, though that would mean placing side by side under consecutive numbers *Christ Washing the Feet of the Apostles*, dated 1754, and the *Adoration of the Shepherds*, which the handling and some extant drawings show to be much later, or mustering before his stay in Rome all his religious pictures though they reveal a thorough knowledge of the Italian masters? Let us agree that as things now stand a comprehensive exhibition and the confrontation of a vast number of works would be the only way to reform the catalogue and establish a reliable chronological order; for sure landmarks are few and far between.

For Boucher's disciple there are none at all. The young artist who at twenty painted the *Jeroboam* now in the Ecole des Beaux-Arts cannot have been satisfied with the few copies after Rembrandt or Van Ostade listed in the catalogues of early sales. The Goncourts mention two prints, *The See-Saw* and *Blind Man's Buff*, that closely resemble Boucher's work, but the inscriptions—at least on a second state—indicate that the originals were painted by Fragonard. They are mawkish pastoral scenes, but in their luxuriant settings one is tempted to recognize the first fruits of Fragonard's brush. One is left in doubt, however, for an examination of the documents leads to utter confusion. Besides these two works, several canvases have been attributed to Fragonard in which we can observe the influence of the artist whose *Shepherd Teaching his Shepherdess to Play the Flute* was exhibited in 1748. Their attribution to Fragonard gives them a glorious name and a high commercial value, but Boucher had a great many disciples and Fragonard a great many talented fellow-pupils. None of these works is signed, and not even the most brilliant shows the slightest sign of Fragonard's future genius. We should be extremely cautious in attributing any of them to him, even the overdoors for the main drawing-room in the Hôtel Matignon, charming pieces the name of whose author is still buried in the archives.

For the Prix de Rome competition in 1752 Fragonard submitted his *Jeroboam Sacrificing to the Idols*, the first picture certainly by his hand. Indeed, in this historical painting Boucher's influence is not greatly in evidence, while there are many reminiscences of Coypel and de Troy. The action is well rendered, the lighting theatrical, the brushwork extremely firm. We can see that the young painter has grasped from the very start the language of his day. His next work, *Psyche Shows her Sisters the Presents She Has Received from Cupid*, executed while he was a pupil of the Ecole des Elèves Protégés and presented to the king in March 1754, has unfortunately been lost. But in that same year Fragonard received a commission for a *Christ Washing the Feet of the Apostles* from the Confraternity of the Blessed Sacrament at Grasse. His fellow-townsmen had not forgotten him; nor, in all probability, had his family. And he may have been recommended by the kindly Van Loo, who was also a native of Provence. The picture is still in Grasse Cathedral. Despite the many vicissitudes it has experienced, we can still recognize a simpler, more austere handling, influenced by seventeenth century models.

We must also regret the loss of the works Fragonard sent home from Rome between 1757 and 1761. His copy of Pietro da Cortona's *St Paul Restored to Sight*, the nudes criticized by Marigny, and the *Head of a Priestess* mentioned by Natoire in a letter of April 1758 have disappeared without leaving a trace. We have, however, some very precise information on that period, proving that it deserves far more consideration than it has received up to now. A substantial number of drawings, such as the charming *Farmyard* in the Ile-de-France Museum at Cap Ferrat, and the volume of engravings by Saint-Non published in 1765 under the title *Raccolta di Vedute Disegnate d'apresso Natura*—three of them by the "little comrade"—reveal a fully developed personality and prove that Fragonard was already Fragonard.

He must have done a lot of work during his last years in Rome. *The Storm* in the Louvre, a dramatic composition, has always been considered one of his most original works: a drawing proves that its conception dates from 1759. The *Little Park* in the Wallace Collection, which is very close to a work engraved by both Saint-Non and Fragonard himself, dates in all likelihood from their stay at Tivoli during the summer of 1760. The same is true of the *View from the Villa d'Este* (now lost, alas!) which Natoire had kept in his collection and of which Saint-Aubin has left us a ghost of a sketch. At the same time as he did these landscapes, Fragonard started on his series of genre pictures with *The Lost Forfeit* (Metropolitan Museum, sketch in the Hermitage) which, according to the catalogue of the Bailli de Breteuil's sale (1786), was painted in Italy, and no doubt *The Preparations for a Meal* (sketch in the Pushkin Museum). Such typically Italian subjects as the two pictures of *Washer-women* (City Art Museum, St. Louis, and Rouen Museum) and the *Italian Family* (Metropolitan Museum), with their chiaroscuro effects and minute accents swiftly touched in with the brush, must date from Fragonard's first stay in Rome (and not from the second, as is generally held); though to please art lovers he may have done replicas of some of them in Paris. In these works the composition reveals the influence of the great Italian models and there is hardly a sign of his personal themes. Yet we can readily understand Natoire's high hopes.

Little is known about Fragonard's production immediately after he returned to France. There is nothing to show that by 1761 he had already become an eager imitator of the Flemish masters and produced only landscapes in the manner of Ruysdael and expressive heads. Particularly as about 1764 we find him very far removed from those formulas and from naturalistic effects. At that time he was busy on the work he submitted to the Academy at the end of March the following year. Two splendid sketches of episodes from the story of Rinaldo and Armida (private collection) have been considered, without the slightest proof, as studies for a picture that was never painted. Why then should they form a pair? It is only the revival of Quinault's opera in 1761 and 1764 that warrants our believing that they are earlier than the major work, *Coresus and Callirrhoe* and the preliminary sketches, the first of which—quite different from the others—is in Angers Museum. The huge canvas, which is conceived in the grand manner and sums up Fragonard's Italian experience tempered by a fresh encounter with the French masters, was a signal success. When it was shown at the 1765 Salon, French painters were in search of new paths and Deshays, on whom great hopes had been

Washerwomen, undated. Oil.

placed, had just died. Like Doyen's *St Genevieve* two years later, Fragonard's *Coresus* seemed destined to usher in a new era of historical painting.

In that same Salon were two drawings of *Views of the Villa d'Este at Tivoli*, doubtless executed earlier, and a *Landscape with a Herdsman Standing on a Knoll* belonging to Bergeret de Grancourt. This work has been lost and there is no way now of deciding whether it was close to *The Storm* or, as one would fain believe, directly reflected the Flemish influence. We must wait until 1772 and Godefroy's two prints entitled *Annette at the Age of Fifteen* and *Annette at the Age of Twenty* to find an important, authenticated reference point in Fragonard's landscape work; though it too is rather vague, for there is every likelihood that the two pictures were painted several years before being popularized as prints. Instead, another picture entitled *The Parents' Absence Turned to*

The Visitation of the Virgin, undated. Pencil and grey wash.

Groups of Children in the Sky ("A Swarm of Cupids"), c. 1765-1767. Oil.

Account, which was submitted after the Salon opened and generally acclaimed, is in the same vein as *The Lost Forfeit*. Fragonard seems to have utilized the most diverse registers and experimented in every direction.

Lenoir claims that *Coresus and Callirrhoe* was immediately followed by a *Visitation* executed for the Duc de Gramont—no doubt the painting we know from sketches now in private collections and the fine drawing in the Ecole Polytechnique in Paris. This work, which still reveals reminiscences of Italy but is so new in its simplicity and the search for a fluid, evanescent poetry, clearly proves what a splendid religious painter Fragonard might have become. At the Salon of 1767 the public expected another brilliant achievement and was disappointed to find only works of minor importance. The round *Head of an Old Man* must have resembled the studies in the Jacquemart-André, Amiens and Nice Museums with their vigorous brushwork, in which Fragonard recalls Rembrandt and still more Rubens and Coypel—fine bits of painting with neither depth nor soul. An oval decorative work "from M. Bergeret's collection" entitled *Groups of Children in the Sky* attracted the wrath of Diderot, who did not mince his words: "an excellent omelette, very soft, very yellow, very well browned." Is this really the oval canvas in the Louvre (Pereire Collection)? We miss the "hundreds of cherubs" mentioned by Diderot, which we find instead in a large oblong wash drawing in Besançon Museum. The latter, a charming work, apparently dates from the same period.

On his return to France, Fragonard seems to have been engaged on a number of large decorative works. The *Groups of Children in the Sky* were doubtless part of a set, but the sketch for a ceiling bequeathed to Besançon Museum by the architect Pâris—and therefore its authenticity is certain—is the only sure example of a production whose loss leaves one of the most serious and irremediable gaps in our knowledge of the painter. Was it not precisely a ceiling piece, for one of the still vacant sections of the Galerie d'Apollon in the Louvre, that the Academy vainly demanded from him in 1766 for his reception by that body?

The next five years were apparently the most active and, on the whole, the best known in the painter's life. We have seen that, thanks to an anecdote recorded by Collé, we can fix 1767 as the date of *The Swing*. Since the *Portrait of M. de la Bretèche* in the Louvre is marked 1769, the "fanciful portraits," whose handling is so peculiar, must have been executed about that time. In June 1770 Drouais sold four overdoors (two of them in Toulon Museum and the Louvre) to Madame du Barry; so those works—more highly finished, and cold for all their deliberate prettiness

—were apparently produced during the same period. The four panels for Louveciennes (Frick Collection, New York) must have been painted between 1770 and 1773. More or less at the same time, Fragonard was working for Mademoiselle Guimard on decorative panels which he left unfinished—young David was called in to complete them—and which are now lost. At forty, Fragonard was at the peak of his career and the apogee of his art. Quick yet perhaps undecided, always charming yet of uneven temper, he turned from the most careful handling to the most daring *fa presto*, from eroticism to mythology and on to vast compositions. The diversity of effects he achieved shows that he was in full possession of his powers. In Paris one trend of painting and taste took him as its exemplar and praised him to the skies; another had already begun to attack him.

It was then, in 1773, that he chose to return to Italy with Bergeret. From that journey we have a large number of drawings, many of them signed and dated, something quite extraordinary for Fragonard. They range from sketches from life recalling mishaps that occurred on the journey to fine drawings in bistre of fairground scenes or parkscapes enlivened by many figures. On his return, at the end of 1774, he must have produced more paintings than ever. But now once again reference points are few and far between and the next thirty years are poorly documented. Though his work won increasing favor with engravers, they often reverted to earlier pictures and—like the sales, where Fragonard's name crops up more and more frequently—afford us no more than a *terminus ante*. It is only because, quite exceptionally, Fragonard inscribed on *The Wardrobe* "entirely by the author's hand" and the date 1778 that we can with some assurance fix the date of that work and assign others of the same type "in the manner of Greuze" to that period. The Salon de la Correspondance, where many of his works were exhibited, usually offered earlier paintings and is of little use for drawing chronological conclusions.

During those years, and even before 1780, Fragonard's art seems to have taken a turn. Tastes were changing rapidly and what people wanted more and more was to be moved. Fragonard slipped into sentimental compositions that extolled conjugal love and the simple joys of family life. One of these is *The Visit to the Foster Mother* (National Gallery, Washington). At the same time his colors grew quieter, his brushwork smoother. The figures fell into line, after the manner of a bas-relief, in the foreground, as in *The Happy Family* (private collection, with sketches). The magic language he had used with such capricious ease became more disciplined and lost one by one its most dazzling tricks. Between 1780 and 1790, in *The Bolt*, *The Stolen Kiss* and *The Contract*, we even find a finished manner and effects borrowed from the most meticulous Dutch painters.

Here too the chronological order is far from clear. But we have proof enough that Fragonard did not wait for the triumph of David and the cold manner to change his style. Compared with Vien, he may have appeared, at the start, as a representative of the opposite trend, but soon he was one of the leaders of the new development. The two drawings in honor of Benjamin Franklin executed in 1778 are still full of fire, yet the handling is already more serious, quieter, even monumental. *The Elements Pay Homage to Nature*, which has disappeared since the Second World War, was dated 1780; though no less lavish than the canvases painted ten or fifteen years earlier, it avoided diagonals and came very close to Vien. In *The Fountain of Love* (Wallace Collection), engraved by Regnault in 1785 and therefore executed before that year, we find simpler volumes outlined by a precise arabesque and profiles borrowed from antiquity. And 1785 was the year David exhibited his *Horatii*, which proclaimed still more clearly, and in a different poetic register, the need for reform.

Fragonard was slightly over fifty and does not give the impression of an artist on the wane or disconcerted by a changing world. He still had twenty years of life before him. And works such as *The Sacrifice of the Rose* and its preliminary sketch (both in private collections), executed before 1793, demonstrate his creative powers. People are too apt to follow Lenoir in saying that the old man had given up painting. Other witnesses tell us he was always hard at work. So this last period, from which scarcely anything has been preserved, may not have been so sterile after all and may still have surprises in store for us.

Thus an œuvre that we think we know so well—while just the contrary is true—comes to a close in a certain obscurity. But if the catalogue is still to be redrafted, the different directions are clear to see. A great variety of genres, a wide range of attitudes, a language that evolves from Boucher, at the start, to Prud'hon and Girodet at the finish, changes of register that lead from boudoir pieces to the most ambitious compositions—that is the essence of Fragonard. That is what debars us from seeing him merely as a Schall possessing genius or a Lavreince who used Rubens' brush. Of his long career the public, and even some historians, recall hardly more than a single period, stretching from *The Swing* to *The Wardrobe*, and a single image, that of a charming painter highlighting a girl's pretty face with a few rosy accents or jotting down indecent drawings with a witty pen. But that period covers no more than twelve years in the life of an artist who wielded the brush for over half a century. It is only a single aspect of the work of a painter who expressed himself in many different ways and found his most personal poetic accents outside the range of these pleasant or titillating works —in the genre scenes of his Roman period, in the landscapes of his maturity, or in the allegories of his old age.

Is this a sign of fertility or indecision? Such diversity might perhaps be censured as resulting from the caprices or frivolity of a genius who had no true bent and scattered his splendid gifts in all directions. Some will see in it the restlessness of a century that had tired of the great philosophical battles it had fought and was poised on the threshold of a violent revolution, the sterile excitement of a society that was making the most of the fading splendors of a way of living and thinking already doomed to disappear. It might perhaps be more interesting to seek in it the incessant labor of a painter who was obsessed by painting and used his freedom in passionately essaying the infinite resources of his language.

The New Model, undated. Oil.

II
THE PAINTER'S LANGUAGE

WHEN Fragonard reached Rome at the end of 1756, he had been preceded by a flattering reputation. His *Jeroboam* had won over the Academy, and Van Loo and Marigny himself saw in the young man the hope of the French School. But very soon Natoire found himself completely at sea. Despite their politely measured terms, the reports he sent to Marigny in Paris barely veil his disappointment. "Fragonard, for all his aptitudes, has an amazing facility for changing his course from one moment to the next; this causes him to work unevenly." A sort of confusion took possession of the young painter when he found himself face to face with Rome and the great masters. He said later that Natoire was so irritated by the inadequacy of the first works he produced there that he even accused him of having deceived the Academy and not being the author of the *Jeroboam*. He threatened to report to Paris on his impression and it was only with the greatest difficulty that Fragonard obtained three months' grace. He spent the time working night and day from models. By degrees he recovered his balance and Natoire's letters began to fill with praise.

The story comes as a complete surprise, for Fragonard gives the impression of being extremely self-confident. But there is another opinion that deserves our notice. It was given by Mariette a few years later, when Fragonard was working on the picture that won him admission to the Academy. "The timidity that predominates in this artist's character stays his hand. Never satisfied with what he does, he continually erases and retouches, which is a method that is very harmful to talent and can injure this young painter. I should be vexed if that happened, for the efforts he makes to do right deserve better success." The idea of Fragonard timid! Then we recall the time he let slip by before submitting his picture to the Academy, the hesitation seemingly attested by the first sketch (Angers Museum), which is so different from the final version.

The statements by men who knew the painter personally throw new light on his creative processes. "L'aimable Frago" always gives the impression of improvising, as if in play or by nature. This facility is an illusion. Recalling the phrase reported by Renouvier, under his passion, his ambition and his tireless effort, we can glimpse his doubts and the will to vie with all his masters. At that time there was certainly no painter who could boast a more thorough culture, none who had sought more deliberately to forge out of that heritage a personal style. Whenever we speak of Fragonard we praise the charm and wit of his canvases. We should perhaps, on the contrary, begin by stressing their science, their style and the boldness of a plastic conception that can bear comparison with the most brilliant that the Baroque age offers in any part of Europe.

The Grand Cascade at Tivoli, from below the Bridge, 1760-1761. Red chalk.

"BOTH A CONNOISSEUR AND A GREAT ARTIST"

(DAVID, 1793)

I F Fragonard ended his career as curator of the Museum, it was no more than his due. David, when nominating him, did not merely help a colleague: he also made a wise choice. One of Fragonard's rare autographs, only recently discovered, shows him in September 1794 giving his expert opinion on a picture offered for sale under the name of Ribera. "On examining it we miss the impasto, the rich, vigorous color, the true, spirited touch with which that able man delighted in painting details... No artist has equalled the facile, clever manner in which the Spagnoletto rendered hands and feet... My recollection of the fine works of that master dictates and upholds an opinion from which it follows that this picture attributed to Ribera called Lo Spagnoletto appears to be a copy made by a very skilful painter."

Ribera, the last artist one would expect Fragonard to care for! In Naples, years before, he had copied the *Lamentation* and other works in the church of the Certosa, but we should hardly have imagined an affinity between that gloomy, tragic follower of Caravaggio and Fragonard's smiling art. What better proof is there that Saint-Non's friend took an interest in all painters, even those whose manner was diametrically opposed to his own. He saw everything, copied everything, remembered everything—France, past and present, Italy from Naples to Venice, Flanders and Holland. Long before the masters of the nineteenth century, he supplemented the comparisons afforded by the great international center that was Paris in his day with a vast search through all Europe, and from it derived an expression that was one of the most decisive ever known to the painter's art.

Already during his apprenticeship years he was in the very heart of painting. At that time Paris was without question the most vital center in Europe. Fragonard, rejected by Chardin and welcomed and initiated by Boucher, was from the start the heir presumptive to that "history painting" in which the tradition of Raphael and the Carracci is blended with the lessons of Poussin and Le Brun, revised after 1670 by the teaching of Rubens—a splendid alloy that David alone succeeded in recasting but only at the cost of destroying it for ever. Fragonard's *Jeroboam* proves that he had mastered all its formulas at the age of twenty.

For he was granted everything at once. From Boucher he learnt all manners and all genres, from heroic nudes to patterned satin skirts, from *chinoiseries* to indoor scenes; from him too he learnt a bright color scheme that frankly juxtaposes warm and cold tones and rejects useful gray for the rainbow's magic. An art at once sensual and gay, that Renoir praised for being pleasant—pleasant to look at and pleasant to practise. Fragonard, who did a copy of *Hercules and Omphale* (sold at the Sireul sale in 1781), never forgot the lesson. But the teaching he received at the Ecole des Elèves Protégés and Van Loo's advice called him back to the examples of the grand manner, as witnessed by his *Christ Washing the Feet of the Apostles* at Grasse. Yet Fragonard was never to be a Baudoin. Moreover, Chardin must have taught him as a boy those tricks of the trade that were the very essence of apprenticeship in the Guild of St Luke. That too had its importance. Fragonard's pictures are well painted and have lost little of their freshness after two centuries.

But for the painters of that age Paris also stood for a tradition that was being increasingly opposed to that of Bologna or Rome. No praise was too great for the genius of Le Sueur and Poussin, virtually all of whose masterpieces were in France at that time. Nor had they quite forgotten Vouet, the painter of woman, the master of bright colors, the real precursor of Boucher. Lagrenée did not hesitate to study La Hyre. Fragonard seems to have paid attention to Bourdon: we can trust the word of Mariette, who was not one to be mistaken on this point. The Bretonvilliers Gallery, dilapidated though it may have been, preserved the glory of a master, many of whose works could still be seen in private collections. Fragonard's *Coresus and Callirrhoe* undoubtedly reflects the lessons he learnt in Italy. But it is from Bourdon, and not from the Bolognese or Neapolitans, that he took the solid pair of columns and the broad step that confine the figures in a strict geometry. It is from Bourdon too that he took the shaft of light that strikes the fair hair and rosy arms of the half-naked infant in the foreground.

But from now on there is no distinguishing between the various lessons Fragonard received. No sooner had he reached Italy than he was stunned by the diversity of the examples he saw. "The energy of Michelangelo terrified me," he said. "I experienced an emotion which I was incapable of expressing; on seeing the beauties of Raphael, I was moved to tears, and the pencil fell from my hand; in the end, I remained for some months in a state of indolence which I lacked the strength to overcome, until I concentrated upon the study of such patterns as permitted the hope that I might one day rival them; it was thus that Barocci, Pietro da Cortona, Solimena and Tiepolo attracted and held my attention."

These remarks were not published by Lenoir until after Fragonard's death, but what he says must be true. There is a letter in which Marigny, commenting on the nude figure study which the young student had just sent in, mentions precisely the first of those names: "It is to be feared that the imitation of some masters may harm him and lead him to adopt affected tones of color . . . One might believe that he has copied Barocci." It is gratifying to meet that painter among Fragonard's first favorites. His delicate, iridescent colors, his wonderful mastery of space, were perfectly attuned to eighteenth-century taste; they blended admirably with the lessons of Rubens while correcting his exaggerated lyricism with a refined, fluid poetry. It is just as easy to see what Fragonard must have admired in Solimena—the grandiose architecture that held him spellbound before his *Heliodorus Driven out of the Temple*, his rapid rhythms and fertile imagination. As for Tiepolo, his every aspect must have pleased Fragonard and been of use to him. As Cochin said, "The great Venetian masters are the true Italian painters." And Boucher too had a collection of drawings by Tiepolo, which Fragonard must have known well. He never forgot the lessons he learnt from Tiepolo's dazzling lights cast on warm tones, his broken arabesque, his shimmering touch, his marvellous combination of grand manner and popular picturesque.

The pupils at the French Academy were obliged to copy one of the pictures in Rome. Fragonard was assigned Pietro da Cortona's *St Paul Restored to Sight* in the church of the Capuchins, which was highly considered at that time and had become famous in a print by Chasteau. Biographers, from Portalis to Grappe, deplore that set piece. The composition seems very austere, it is true; but what painter could have been closer in spirit to Fragonard? The delicacy of Pietro da Cortona's female figures, their raven locks contrasting with milky-white brows, the quivering rhythm that conjures up sensual pleasure and license, captivated Prud'hon who, when allotted the task of copying the Barberini ceiling, composed the fine work we admire today in the Palais des Etats at Dijon. Fragonard must have given no less consideration to that masterpiece and to all the other paintings in Rome and Florence by an artist who will always be one of those best calculated to fascinate the French. But we may rest assured that he did not disregard the other masters whose works fill the churches of Rome. The trip to Naples with Saint-Non, their journey back to Paris via Bologna, Venice and Genoa, and later the veritable artistic expedition organized by Bergeret, served to complete his repertory. Fragonard saw and studied the whole range of Italian painting, and copied much of it. The *Fragments choisis* list a great

Washerwomen, c. 1758-1761. Oil.

variety of names, from Caravaggio to Tornioli, from Albani to Luca Giordano, and from Ghirlandajo to Pietro della Vecchia.

There has been discussion, even dispute, as to whether Fragonard's long years in Italy were balanced by a trip to the Low Countries. Some demur because no source gives direct mention of it. Others insist on the obvious influence of northern painting. No irrefutable fact has yet cropped up that might decide the issue. Considering how few documents on Fragonard's life have been preserved, we are less surprised to find no mention of a journey that may have been quite short. But why is there not a single drawing of northern landscapes when we have so many views of Italy? Portalis thought he had found a decisive argument in a *Study of a Mill* in sepia (Grasse Museum). But in those days the

The Cradle, undated. Oil.

smallest village could boast a mill and it would have to be proved that this one, which reappears in the landscape called *The Return of the Herd* (Worcester Art Museum), is beyond doubt a mill in Holland and was not simply copied from some Dutch painting. Far more weighty is the series of drawings that are direct copies of Dutch or Flemish masterpieces and were already included in the sale of the Gros Collection in April 1778. Would a wash drawing of Jordaens' *Triumph of the Prince of Orange* (private collection, Paris) have fetched five hundred livres and one of Rembrandt's *Night Watch* (lost) six hundred had they been no more than copies of copies? So it is only extreme caution that prevents us from accepting the hypothesis as actual fact.

It is really of no great importance. "Fashion," Caylus exclaimed addressing the Academy, "has almost banished Italy from our cabinets and nowadays offers us nothing but Flemings." At Boucher's sale, Fragonard himself bought a *Portrait of a Burgomaster* by Van Dyck, 69 drawings by Rembrandt and his school, and 292 prints of Dutch and Flemish masters. We should like to know that he experienced the revelation of Rembrandt before the *Night Watch* itself and discovered Rubens in the churches of Antwerp. But it was at Crozat's that, while still an apprentice, he had done the copy of Rembrandt's *Infant Jesus Asleep* (Hermitage) that appeared in Boucher's sale in 1771. And it was in the Luxembourg that he studied the craftsmanship of Rubens, as witnessed by a note from Cochin dated October 1767, asking Marigny to obtain for Fragonard and Baudoin permission to consult the master's pictures whenever they liked.

We should not be surprised by his choice. For about a hundred years painters had idolized Rubens, and Rembrandt's fame was reaching the point where he rivaled the supremacy of the masters of Rome and Bologna. But the contrast between the two should not be overlooked: Rembrandt stood, first and foremost, for tonal values and the rejection of a colorful palette; Rubens instead for modeling with color, the endeavor to achieve a higher tonality and show the blood coursing under the skin. Here again Fragonard hesitated, then took something from each. *The Cradle* (Amiens Museum) has the same contrasted lighting as Rembrandt's *Infant Jesus Asleep*, while in *The Little Preacher* (private collection) we find the rosy modeling, heightened with vermilion in the shadows, touched with white in the high-lights and with blue-gray in the half-tones, which is Rubens's most personal lesson. It reoccurs, triumphant, in the *Women Bathing* in the Louvre.

We must not, however, believe that Fragonard learnt from those two masters only. If he carefully copied Rembrandt's *Ganymede* and *Self-Portraits*, he paid no less attention to Van Eeckhout's *Boy Reading* (sepia wash, Cognacq-Jay Museum, Paris). As for Frans Hals, now that we know more about the resources of Italy, we are less inclined than

Landscape with Washerwomen, undated. Oil.

were Pierre de Nolhac and Louis Réau to decide that the "fanciful portraits" necessarily derive from Hals. After all, a close study of Tintoretto or Johann Liss would have sufficed. But the landscape painters of the Low Countries certainly held his attention. Fragonard perhaps first saw nature through Boucher's eyes, but he felt its direct impact again in Italy in the company of Hubert Robert. There he took to heart the lessons of Castiglione, whose huddled flocks mingle with the vast, wild sky in *The Storm*. Back in Paris, he seems, like all his contemporaries, to have admired the Dutch masters, from Ruysdael to Hobbema, and subtly combined their example with his Italian experience.

The Storm, c. 1759. Oil.

This influence is reflected in a large number of works. Some are veritable *pastiches*, with a vast sky that fills most of the canvas, low-lying plains, and hillocks whose tortured trees and thickets are silhouetted against the clouds. There are several authenticated examples, including *The Watering Place* and *The Rock* (Veil-Picard Collection) and the fine *Landscape with Washerwomen* (Grasse Museum) that once belonged to Louis XVIII. But we must take care not to exaggerate their number for, then and later, Lantara, Bruandet and many other painters showed an equal interest in the Dutch masters. At the same time Fragonard studied the minor masters of genre painting, from Van Ostade to Mieris, as witnessed by the two diminutive panels, *Young Couple at the Window* and *Young Mother and Her Child*, in Besançon Museum. Late in life, reverting to a more finished handling, he even imitated the interiors of Metsu and Ter Borch and their sumptuous satin gowns. It has often been repeated that *The Stolen Kiss* points the way to Boilly; but if this new trend, with its still-life arrangement of a striped scarf and a handful of ribbons on a small round table and a door half-open on a delicately toned-down interior, pays homage to Metsu, does it not also recall Fragonard's first master, Chardin?

Thus one aspect of Fragonard's œuvre shows him looking to the past, to those "museums" which then did not yet exist and which he not much later helped to set up. "He was an inspired *pasticheur*," said the Goncourts, "who had always with him, even in his most intimate moments, the memory and the support of this familiarity with the technique of his masters." Yet not even the historians who are most ready to talk of eclecticism have ever reproached Fragonard for that. From then on, the knowledge of the connoisseur risked being a danger for the painter. It was the ruin of so many others—Lantara, Boissieu and that charming master so close at times to Fragonard, Norblin de la Gourdaine, whom we can only get to know properly in Poland or from his graphic work. Fragonard succeeded in evading the temptation. Such were the resources of this Southerner, who appreciated the works of the past but loved life and the present too much to seek refuge in them.

The Stolen Kiss, before 1788. Oil.

The Stolen Kiss (detail), before 1788. Oil.

In fact, a refuge was the last thing Fragonard was interested in. No painter has ever cared less for seclusion or lived more in the midst of his fellows. It is impossible to name all those whom he met and may have been influenced by. We know that in Rome he was on intimate terms with Greuze, who had arrived there not long before with the Abbé Gougenot and whose example often haunted him. And there, above all, he met Hubert Robert, the French ambassador's brilliant protégé, who had been admitted to the Academy even though he had never even competed for the Prix de Rome. The influence these two painters had on each other cannot be overemphasized. In some ways they were very different; Robert was a sturdy young fellow, five feet four, highly cultivated and in easy circumstances. But both were sociable, easygoing, yet hard-working. They at once became close friends, and to the very end the lives and characters of the two men run curiously parallel. Fragonard was a year older but Robert had already spent five years in Rome and enjoyed a certain prestige, both in artistic circles and in society, in which he shone. No doubt the newcomer fell under his spell, but Robert too may have found that there was much to be learnt from Boucher's pupil, trained in the great tradition of history painting. Their manner of drawing and painting must for a time have been quite similar, and Fragonard's Italian works will not be fully understood until a thorough study of Robert's work has been made. And this applies not only to the landscapes, for which Fragonard seems to have acquired a taste from his friend; a canvas like Robert's *Italian Farm* (Kervéguen Collection) is inseparably linked with Fragonard's interiors, and the *Rustic Kitchen* exhibited under Fragonard's name in Moscow Museum (though unmentioned in any of the catalogues) cannot be studied without reference to their common researches.

Fragonard's relations with other painters in Rome, and later in Paris, must also be taken into account; but here, while many names are linked with his, few particulars have been recorded. It would be hard to prove that he was in personal contact with Mengs or Batoni; but is it reasonable to assume that, in over four years spent in Rome, he closed his eyes to their work and took no notice of the trends developing there at the time, even if they were uncongenial to him? In Paris, he lived in the Louvre surrounded by other artists, all of whom knew him, by art lovers and by dealers. And when at last age might have led to isolation, his son was there to bring home—not, it seems, without a dash of fanaticism—all the latest ideas.

It is not surprising, therefore, that if the masters of the past long held Fragonard's attention, they never dominated him. Even in Rome the prejudices of the *cognoscenti* did not prevent his being immediately attracted by movement, expression and color. The *Fragments choisis* are not an impartial anthology. Poussin is represented not by his revered masterpieces, but by the first works he did in Rome: the charming *Bacchanal of Children* in the Chigi Palace, *The Massacre of the Innocents* with its grandiose tragic effect, and the copy of *The Triumph of Flora* still in the Campidoglio. Lodovico Carracci rivals Annibale, while Sebastiano Ricci occupies more space than Titian. And among the host of great Venetians, Fragonard went straight for *The Vision of St Jerome* by Johann Liss, who was the least famous of them all but displays, a hundred years in advance, all the shimmer and "dishevelment" of the eighteenth century.

That also explains his attitude towards the ancients. Through Saint-Non and his other friends, Fragonard was in direct contact with the circle of *curieux* whose one ambition was the restoration of antiquity, from Caylus in Paris to the Italian scholar Paciaudi whom he must have met in Rome. From them Vien learnt a new lesson and derived the formulas of a style that evoked universal applause. Fragonard did nothing of the sort. In his eyes antiquity was not imbued with magic. He enjoyed ruins for their contrast with the commonplace, which gives Rome and Naples such charm. But he refused to seek lessons for his painting in ancient statues or even in the few frescoes that were being unearthed at that time. Despite his long stay in Italy, he did not become a leader of the trend that preached a reversion to the antique and took Winckelmann's writings for its Bible. In the little set of *Bacchanalia* he etched himself, he followed, after more than a hundred years, the trail blazed by the charming Brébiette. Antique bas-reliefs furnished the pretext, but his bacchantes and satyrs, animated in turn by amorous or domestic sentiments, dance and play in absolute liberty. The needle, by a profusion of light touches crisscrossing in all directions, makes the whole sheet vibrate after the manner of Castiglione and the Venetians.

His was the antiquity of Tiepolo or, if you prefer, of Clodion. But the set is dated 1763, the year in which Vien exhibited his *Marchande d'Amours* in the Salon.

Fragonard was too much in love with life to become a genuine antiquary. He was a connoisseur who never tired of turning back to nature. The eighteenth century always taught that an artist must refer back to nature first and last. Even the artful Boucher never ceased copying from the model and advising his pupils to do the same. Fragonard followed his precept all his life long. We have seen that in Rome, overcome (and perhaps, in some respects, disappointed) by his encounter with the great masters, he concentrated for three months on studying from nature and so recovered his balance. He copied Guido Reni and Pietro da Cortona but also scoured the countryside with his portfolio under his arm, and went to work at Tivoli with Hubert Robert. The hand that delighted in over-pretty female profiles sketched the *Beggar with Wallet* (private collection), of which Mariette noted—undeservedly, of course—in the margin of the catalogue of the Huquier sale in 1772: "He will never do anything better." This explains how it is that his work, despite moments of complacency and a dangerous inclination to indulge in pleasing conventions, never shows a trace of routine. It also explains the freshness and diversity revealed in that work at the very time when Fragonard was carried away by the most daring plastic researches.

Portrait of a Horseman ("Saint-Non in Spanish Costume"), c. 1769. Oil.

"PAINTED IN AN HOUR'S TIME"

(PORTRAIT OF LA BRETÈCHE, LOUVRE)

I N the inventory of the Hall collection, compiled in 1778, we find this note under Fragonard's name: "A head after myself at the time when he did portraits in a single sitting for a louis." The picture in question has not been recovered, but there is every reason to believe it was one of the series of so-called "fanciful portraits" of which some fifteen are known today and to which Charles Sterling has devoted a masterly study. Two of the most striking were till lately in the Château de Champ-de-Bataille and had always belonged to the d'Harcourt family, who looked upon them as likenesses of the Comte François-Henri and Marquis Anne-François. Another, in the Rothschild collection, owes its title of *The Actor* to the swaggering pose. A fourth, discovered more recently, was purchased by the Sterling and Francine Clark Art Institute, Williamstown, Massachusetts. The sitter, a dry, severe old man, is quaintly dressed up as a sort of Don Quixote, complete with ruff, doublet and martial bearing. The most complete series is in the Louvre, thanks to the generosity of Louis La Caze and Carlos de Beistegui. On the back of one is the following inscription in an old-fashioned hand: "Portrait of La Bretèche, painted by Fragonard, in 1769, in an hour's

Portrait of a Man ("The Warrior"), c. 1769. Oil.

time." There seems no reason to doubt this statement, and one at least of the other male portraits in the Louvre may well represent the Abbé de Saint-Non (La Bretèche's brother), though it is not easy to recognize in these dandies his delicate temperament and the profile, in an etching dated 1766, which is said to represent him.

Portrait of La Bretèche ("Music"), 1769. Oil.

Are these portraits or pretexts? Everything tends to make us forget the model. There is no setting to place him, and only in one of these pictures, known as *The Abbé de Saint-Non in Spanish Costume* (Museum of Fine Arts, Barcelona), is the figure depicted at full length before the silhouette of a horse. Nor are there any symbols to designate the model halfway between speech and a smile. The demeanor of an absent-minded interlocutor or a hectoring braggart with brandished fist and puffed-out chest tells us nothing about a man's character—at least nothing that is not borrowed from the stage. The hands, a few streaks of pigment, have no more expression than the crumpled gloves slipped between their fingers. But a gust of wind ruffles the silks and stirs the hair; a brusque gesture twists the silhouette and shifts the direction of the gaze. Something is held prisoner in these pictures—the fleeting moment.

Many other artists have sought to achieve the same effect, first among them Rubens, the Venetians, Frans Hals and Velazquez. Bernini dreamt of doing it in marble. Fragonard outstripped them all. Or rather, he skipped, garbled, scribbled what he lacked the time to paint. A few swaths of red suffice to suggest a cloak that snaps and flaps as none ever did in a gale (*Portrait of Saint-Non*, Louvre). A patch of vermilion curdles on the cheek-bones or the tip of a blotchy nose (d'Harcourt portraits). Plausibility is completely forgotten. There can be no question of catching the sitter in the fleeting expression that sums up a face, as Bernini did. Nor of avoiding an intellectual image while rendering the appearance of life and its very essence. The brush sweeps at headlong speed: that is what really counts. Speed has become an end to itself.

This art has its limits. However great the painter's virtuosity may be, there are times when speed leaves no more than a senseless trail. The imagination fails to respond to the ill-applied spur; the hand writes at haphazard and what we read is tedious chitchat. In Fragonard we find this particularly in some drawings where we feel only too clearly that the desire to please is all that animates a brilliant but banal scene. The whole corpus of his drawings—which there is no question of studying in this book—contains some magnificent sheets in which the language is concise and to the point; others display an excessive carelessness. At the Exhibition of French Drawing from Fouquet to Cézanne in 1950, André Lhote was vexed to see *The Pasha*, one of Fragonard's occasional *turqueries* and not by any means the best, hailed as a masterpiece. "Nothing," Lhote growled, "could give a better idea of the decadence of art; the

Inspiration, undated. Oil.

Women Bathing, undated. Oil.

"SLAPPED ON, DASHED OFF,
WELL WHIPPED UP"

(Dialogues on Painting, 1773)

Go to the Louvre and admire Boucher's *Rest of Diana*; it is a small picture, yet one of his masterpieces and hardly excelled by any but *The Triumph of Amphitrite* in Stockholm. In it we find all the grace of the eighteenth century and all the science of an art that uses a bright range of color to delight our eyes. Then turn to Fragonard's *Women Bathing*: something is different, but it is neither the grace nor the Rubensian feeling for color. It goes deeper.

First give yourself up to the pleasure of this medley of tints, deep pink, amber, ash green; this inextricable mingling of nude bodies, foaming water and foliage. Now pull yourself together. It will take you a few moments to perceive the logic of the scene. You did not at once discern the tree that has fallen across the stream, and across the picture, of which it is, so to say, the pretext and the key. Little by little, you distinguish one bank from the other, the leaves from the sky, the reeds from the roots and the drapery. Two clumps of greenery become articulated, mingled with blues and earths, separated by a broad diagonal in which all the warm tones are concentrated: the golden or milky-white bodies of the bathers, the rosy drapery heightened by a few touches of vermilion. You cannot fail to see that the picture is first and foremost just that—a bouquet of colors. A charming subject, no doubt, and one that obviously seeks to please. But it is not representation. Here who cares about plausibility? The fallen tree, the curving reeds, the bodies that slide or tumble —they all elude not only staticity but also that other force of gravity which is reality. These reeds are not reeds but streaks of pigment; these drapes that take wing without cause at the slightest puff of wind are first and foremost a few slashes of pink and white. A nimble brush has borrowed from the sky the shadow on leg or bosom, and drawn from the water's depth the transparent modeling. The painter's hand seems to race along, the forms to rise before our eyes, the rhythms to fill the canvas. That is the picture—no longer the representation of a spectacle, but a tapestry woven from one end to the other with the same silky skeins.

We are apt to believe that all "pure" painting must be "flat" painting. Maurice Denis's famous formula convinces us that the pleasure of painting only arises at the moment when the picture "becomes a flat surface covered with colors arranged in a certain order." That, in truth, was the admirable theory of the Nabis, who in this respect followed the trail blazed by Manet. But it is important to feel (as some abstract painting nowadays makes us feel) that the play of colors and forms can be organized in a dynamic space. I would go so far as to distinguish between two schools of thought that are equally ready to exalt handling and combine patches of color. One prefers the surface of the canvas, the other the space within the picture. This can be inferred without difficulty from the works of conventional painters, some of whom compose by cutting up the picture plane, while others think first of the dynamic relationships that will occupy the depth of the scene. Tintoretto, Tiepolo, the Neapolitan decorators and Rubens are masters of the latter trend. Fragonard sided with them, and a painting like his *Women Bathing* is a perfect example of this play of colors and forms attuned to spatial research.

Here we have the extreme expression of that "baroque" vision long since analysed by Wölfflin, the moment when it works itself up into a

Rinaldo in Armida's Garden, undated. Oil.

paroxysm and pushes illusion to the point of self-destruction. No pictures are more revealing in this respect than the two scenes from the story of Rinaldo and Armida—unless, perhaps, at the other end of Europe, with totally different aims and based chiefly on the play of values, certain works by Maulbertsch. Here again Fragonard has borrowed his subject from the theater and the composition is operatic. The hero advances towards the center of the stage surrounded by props and by cleverly arranged supers. In one canvas the focal point is a large blue hole filled with ill-defined forms; in the other it is the huge, slanting tree planted in the middle of the picture. A series of diagonals breaks the spatial logic; there are no sure reference points for the eye, no certainty for the mind. A mass of brief indications lead the eye towards indistinct depths and draw it from one side of the canvas to the other. The color adds to the confusion, for the brush refuses subservience to the object it depicts. Rinaldo and Armida are mere puppets, they have neither features nor expression. The other figures dissolve in cleverly distributed warm and cold masses. But the artist's hand moves on deftly. From an almost abstract medley there emerges a head, a body, a plume. Hastily the brush, with a few touches of Prussian blue, pure vermilion and yellow ochre, which suggest as if by chance an occasional silhouette, covers the canvas with a uniformly rapid rhythm that casts a musical spell over the spectator. Thus the "painterly" vision, as defined by Wölfflin, which rejects stable forms, tactile values and intellectual clarity, is pushed to its ultimate consequences. But, by a singular inversion, what elsewhere tends to strengthen the fiction here ends up by annulling it and results in an entirely new art.

These two pictures occupy an extremely important place in French painting, for never before had it sought so clearly to free itself from the trammels of the subject and surrender to the pure pleasure of the brush. We must bear in mind the state of the French School at that time. With Boucher an old man and Van Loo about to pass away, a need for renovation was making itself felt on every side. But the trends were still confused. Some placed the accent on style and handling; others insisted on lofty subjects and noble inspiration. All extolled "grand taste" and the "grand manner," but none defined them very clearly. Vien was hailed as the man who restored Greek "purity" and "simplicity." But high hopes were also placed in the realism of Deshays and Doyen, a well as in the dramatic poetry, the dream effect in which pathos blends with fantasy that Diderot thought he saw in Fragonard's *Coresus*. This confusion long justified the belief that the call to revert to a "noble," "severe" style came from the reactionaries; and a "modern party," attuned to the taste of art lovers, sought instead to expand the resources of painting. It was not until 1770 or thereabouts that a new trend appeared which to this painting for pleasure opposed a more thoughtful art based on the example of Poussin and Le Sueur.

At that time Fragonard was considered the most brilliant representative of "free," "bold" painting, along with Hallé, Doyen, Brenet and Taraval. The four panels he executed for Louveciennes (or Lussienne, as it was called in those days) were a deliberate attempt to produce an exceptionally large-scale decoration which should combine brilliant handling with "modern" poetry yet evade the "trivial manner." The artist's contemporaries apparently realized this. He was admired and attacked. I shall have more to say about these works, but let me quote here an anonymous *Dialogue sur la peinture* published in 1773, which may give us an idea of the reputation Fragonard enjoyed at the time and the importance of the masterpiece.

"You have seen at Lussienne," says one of the fictitious interlocutors, "the *nec plus ultra* in the slapped on, dashed off, well whipped up. There, that is the real daub."

"Dashed on, well whipped up, daub! Do you mean that as insult . . . or praise?"

"What! You must be quizzing me! I am talking about the divine Fragr., the most capital brush, say the arbiters of our painting. That fellow lacks nothing. One of these days friend Foliot is to publish a treatise in which he proves at great length that the divine Fragr. is Michelangelo and Titian rolled into one."

Rinaldo in the Magic Forest, undated. Oil.

"Well, Monsieur Fragr., with all due respect to the writer, the friends of Michelangelo and Titian will never be yours..."

"But he has made a reputation with the financiers, and for a painter that is as good as any. One says he is Raphael; another calls him Guercino. All their cabinets are adorned with his works."

"Such customers do not surprise me, and Midas, good old Midas, can appoint him his premier painter..."

Did Madame du Barry, who commissioned the decoration, feel this last taunt? Winckelmann's theories, which reached Paris in 1775, were beginning to bear fruit. For the pavilion at Louveciennes, Ledoux had chosen an architecture inspired by the severest antiquity. The fact that a set of panels by Vien replaced Fragonard's, whatever the reason may have been, assumes a symbolic significance.

Fragonard must have realized that himself. For this style is found in only a few pictures painted within quite a brief period; they reveal the extent of the artist's researches but are not the sum total of his œuvre. After 1775 we see him revert little by little to well-defined volumes enclosed in a clearly drawn outline and his brush grows more discreet. I said before that the splendid *Fountain of Love* in the Wallace Collection already displays David's solid forms. *The Oath of the Horatii* propounded

Rinaldo in the Magic Forest (detail), undated. Oil.

a formula that was diametrically opposed to that of the Louveciennes panels and the pictures of Rinaldo and Armida. But Fragonard had not waited for David to show him the way.

So this grand "baroque" language is like the last wonderful, tardy blossom of a long tradition. But genius always comes into its own. Long after David, the brush that neglected modeling, covered the canvas with the same rapid accents or left behind long swaths of color, influenced Daumier—a totally unexpected happening pointed out by Charles Sterling. It has made an impact on all modern painting bent on diverting interest from representation to the painterly substance. And it is only the charm of Fragonard's subject matter, which still troubles our contemporaries, that prevents his name being added to those of the great precursors—Rubens, Hals, Goya, Delacroix—mentioned by Malraux in his *Voices of Silence*.

III
FRAGONARD, THE LYRIC POET

The Bed of State, undated. Pen and ink wash
heightened with watercolor on white paper.

"Do you remember all those mischievous little cupids with their saucy naked bottoms, barely visible high up in the sky of *The Embarkment for Cythera*? Where are they off to? They are going to play at Fragonard's and shed the dust from their butterfly wings onto his palette."

A pretty conceit, and true enough as far as it goes. But it does not go far enough. The Goncourts were referring to one of Fragonard's artistic sponsors—but only one, and perhaps the one most apt to blind us to his true personality. What struck those realistic novelists most in the eighteenth century was the amorous banter and the shepherdesses in furbelows. It is perfectly true that Watteau's *putti*, after stopping off at Boucher's, went on to Fragonard's to tug at one girl's nightgown (*The Stolen Shift*, Louvre) or trouble another's sleep (*All Ablaze*, Louvre). But we would search for them in vain in *The Fête at Rambouillet*. Is it they or —for all their pretty dimples—already some of their romantic cousins, that haunt *The Fountain of Love*?

We must bear in mind that Fragonard's eighteenth century is no longer the eighteenth century of carefree gaiety. Fragonard was born in

offered novelists a thousand piquant plots. So they took the other line, which writers, being too much concerned with wit to tarry over description, mostly left to the reader's imagination. It was the brush's task to depict physical charms, even the most immodestly displayed, and amorous fervor, even beyond the limits of propriety. Boucher had set the example, but Fragonard was the best exponent of what may be called boudoir painting.

There we find the lilies and the roses, the little tip-tilted nose, the furbelows that barely veil and the veils that conceal nothing. And the type of woman who symbolizes in our eyes the charm of that age. The noble profiles of antiquity or the seventeenth century and their blonde, fleshy beauties are relegated to grand tragic roles.

> Seventeen years, a nymph-like figure,
> Large sloe-black eyes that brim with fun;
> Her talk is small, but charms me ever;
> My head's been turned by such a one.

The Chevalier de Bonnard's doggerel is a perfect description of the Baron de Saint-Julien's belle on her swing.

There was hardly a major French painter, with the exception of Le Brun, who did not pay his tribute to feminine beauty. But none could rival Fragonard in that respect. Boucher is repetitive; Ingres strives to keep his dignity. Fragonard, instead, gives his delight free rein; he multiplies and improvises with true southern gaiety. From society beauties to country lassies. In the *Girl Reading* he dwells on the rounded chin of a child; in *The Bolt* he shows us the supple, willowy figure of a girl of twenty. Above all, his brush never limned a plain woman. The vogue for things eastern was a pretext for depicting innumerable bearded old men with a Semitic cast of features, but he was unable to age a woman's face. It is with obvious regret that he added, here and there, an accent of bistre or a touch of powder, like a make-up man obliged to disguise a pretty woman as a duenna. In *The New Model* (Jacquemart-André Museum, Paris) the pandering mother seems just old enough to be her daughter's elder sister; and in *The Visitation* St Elizabeth is very nearly as young as the Virgin Mary. His men, too, are lay figures with the physique of hoary beaux or namby-pamby juvenile leads. Consider the fine, free study in the museum at Le Havre, copied perhaps from some Italian model: all Fragonard could use it for is the mawkish actor in *The Happy Family* (private collection). There came a day when David painted *Leonidas at Thermopylae*, a paean to masculine beauty without a single female figure to enliven it. Probably he could not have done so if Fragonard had not so brilliantly and so truly extolled woman's charms.

His praises are slightly insistent at times. So many dark-eyed glances, so many archly pretty faces, are rather too suggestive. And one does not

The Longed-for Moment, undated. Oil.

The Stolen Shift, undated. Oil.

have to be a sanctimonious puritan to be shocked. *The Overturned Chair* (bistre wash, private collection) and *Seamstresses Going to Bed* (sepia, Fogg Art Museum, Cambridge) hardly attempt to mask their impropriety. *The Useless Resistance* (National Museum, Stockholm), with its rumpled pillow, unlaced bodice and flaunted garter, borders on the erotic. A jaded palate is not satisfied with grace; it demands the flush of surprise, the relaxation of early morning, the frolics of two pretty girls, the disordered bed that holds a promise—or a memory. When we think of the scrupulous modesty of the nineteenth century, we are not surprised at the disappearance of quite a large number of these paintings, which we know chiefly from prints or drawings.

Yet there is nothing morbid in them. Handsome lads kiss buxom lasses, who put up no resistance. We are far removed, indeed, from Sade or even Laclos. Fragonard is indiscreet, but his indiscretion is preferable to some veiled allusions. It was Baudoin who drew *The Empty Quiver* and a host of small compositions that do not shock the eye but in the long run irritate us with their *double entendre*, just as Diderot's *Bijoux Indiscrets* soon raises a yawn. Fragonard instead painted *The Kiss* and *The Longed-for Moment* (private collections) and gives more pleasure because he makes less fuss.

In his work we see frankness and health—even, I would like to say, a certain innocence. That is because his women are young girls who

All Ablaze, undated. Oil.

Making Love in a Cowshed, undated. Bistre wash.

blush at their first experience of love, his lovers are youths who show more boldness than they really feel. Even in *The Orgy* (bistre wash, Boymans-Van Beuningen Museum, Rotterdam), perhaps his most improper drawing, the scene is set in a world of adolescents, where the characters are called Fanny, Susie or Jack, where kisses are given as forfeits (*The Lost Forfeit*, Metropolitan Museum), and lovers embrace in dark corners when younger brothers are looking the other way (*The Parents' Absence Turned to Account*, Hermitage). *Fireworks* and *Aquatic Sports*, which we know only from Auvray's prints, are set in a dormitory where surprise chances to disclose a bosom here, there a chubby bottom, or even more; but the face that appears at the trapdoor is not that of Susanna's lecherous elders. "I would ask the reader to bear in mind that I am only twenty-five years old," says the hero of *Point de Lendemain*, "and that one is not bound by what one does at that age." The painter enjoys the same privilege. Youth and beauty make free with morals; sin only makes its appearance with the first wrinkle.

But Frago's womenfolk never show a wrinkle. Reality threatens them still less than age. A pretty face, a smooth skin, a perfect figure —that is not the convention of ancient sculpture, accepted with enthusiasm by the previous century, but an ideal which, though modern and piquant, was none the less an abstraction. Observe, in the Louvre, *All Ablaze*, certainly a very daring subject with Cupid lighting the target all too clearly with his torch. Then pass on to Courbet's *Women Sleeping*, the gem of the Petit-Palais, and consider their heavy sleep, their fleshy chins, their skin clammy with nasty sweat. You will agree that the indecency is not in Fragonard's work. His characters never possess the weight of reality, the dangerous force of emotion that gives scandal. A uniform grace, the lightness of an allusion, even the brush, which does not finish but is content to suggest without describing—all help to remind us that the world we are looking at exists only in painting. A gracious world inhabited by lively minor deities whose chief occupation is to please and win over; a happy world where original sin is as far away as in the days of the Renaissance.

The Hollyhocks, 1790-1791. Decorative panel. Oil.

LOFTY LYRIC ACCENTS

Is there any point of contact between Chénier's pleasing verses and the carnal hymn of Rubens or even Renoir's joyous gluttony? There is, no doubt, something that distinguishes Fragonard from Schall and Lavreince, on the one hand, and from Greuze and Boilly on the other. The difference, we are told, is in the free play of the brush rather than in the inspiration. But we must not let ourselves be taken in by the good fellow, so gay, so sociable, seemingly as artless as a child, without a secret to his name, who yet one day confessed to Bergeret that he always said not what he thought but what he thought would please.

No doubt the *Girl Dancing Her Dog on Her Bed* (private collection) is merely the masterpiece of a minor painter; but the same cannot be said of *The Longed-for Moment*. Here unessentials dissolve, pretexts vanish. All that remains is a couple, an embrace, less still: a moment of passion. Who had ever depicted that so fearlessly, without a mythological pretext, without involving Mars and Venus or Diana and Endymion? André Chénier dared to later, when he described a couple embracing:

> Two young breasts cleave and throb as one,
> Two pairs of lips joined by one fire
> Mingle sweet labor, sighs of desire,
> And greedy, moist, delicious kisses . . .

Storming the Citadel, between 1770 and 1773. Oil.

The very fact that the comparison is feasible gives the measure of Fragonard. How far removed here from Lavreince! Of course, our time, which dotes on tragedy and desolation, prefers Picasso's *The Embrace*. But is there more true humanity in the isolation of two poor souls than in the exaltation of two young bodies? The century of enlightenment believed in happiness.

The Pursuit, between 1770 and 1773. Oil.

Storming the Citadel (detail), between 1770 and 1773. Oil.

Let us glance through Fragonard's drawings. His illustrations for La Fontaine's *Contes* are charming sketches on trivial subjects. We are irritated that he chose so tedious and prosy a work, whose licentiousness pleased a century that placed Voltaire's *La Pucelle* among man's loftiest achievements. Fragonard wittily glossed over smutty details but his nimble handling and subtle composition give those sheets a peculiar charm. The Cognacq-Jay Museum has a drawing entitled *Making Love in a Cowshed*. Observing this rustic scene, who would think of Boucher's *The Cage* or his *Amorous Shepherd*? A lad tumbles a suddenly scared lass in the straw; the scene is depicted without brutality or reticence. Here the old story of "Il pleut, il pleut, bergère..." is told without mawkish compliments or snowy sheep. Alone a huge white bull observes the scene with a hostile eye. The strong masculinity of the bull held a curious fascination for Fragonard, who employed the motif repeatedly. We see it in the cowshed, massive and motionless, or raising its slobbering muzzle to eye the herdsman as he embraces his sweetheart leaning against the edge of the trough, or watching like some rustic deity over the girl asleep in the hay. There is no reason to imagine some psychoanalytical overtone: the allusion is perfectly clear. But Lavreince chose suggestive symbols—mouse or flea—while Greuze dwelt on dead birds and broken pitchers. There we have the distance that separates real poetry from literature.

Even in Fragonard's love scenes we are shown the other aspect of his œuvre. He seemed merely more brilliant and more skilful than the others; we find him different. He seemed simple and gay; we find him profound. Suddenly he evades the theme or oversteps it. Suddenly the fashionable painter of erotica goes to the roots of love. A visionary peeps out from behind the decorator of boudoirs.

The panels in the Frick Collection, in New York, were meant to be drawing-room decorations. We have already seen that Madame du Barry ordered them for her pavilion at Louveciennes and that documentary evidence proves that they were executed between 1770 and 1773. For some unknown reason, they remained only a short time in their allotted place (or perhaps were never set up at all) and Vien was commissioned to paint four others to replace them. Historians have said that some details displeased the king's mistress, or maybe the king himself who, they suggest, recognized himself in the figure of the lover. Others pretend that the canvases were too large for the frames. I am more tempted to admit, with Franklin M. Biebel, that the pictures seemed too

The Declaration of Love, or The Souvenirs,
or The Love Letter, between 1770 and 1773. Oil.

The Lover Crowned, between 1770 and 1773. Oil.

much at variance with the prevailing architectural style of Ledoux's neoclassical pavilion; and Fragonard was not the man to accept criticism. In any case, he took back his canvases and kept them in his possession; the family said he had never consented to explain exactly what happened. When he betook himself to Grasse in 1790, he had them sent on after him, fearing perhaps that they might remain rolled up indefinitely

The Lover Crowned (detail), between 1770 and 1773. Oil.

and get lost. This point is worth recalling for it shows what store he set by these works. He arranged them in the drawing-room in the house of his cousins the Mauberts, and to complete the decoration added a fifth episode that concluded the adventure on a moral note, in keeping with the taste of the day, and a whole set of panels representing cupids and hollyhocks that bring to mind Renoir. The whole remained intact in the hands of the Maubert family until the end of the nineteenth century, but even the account of it written by Portalis could not save it for France. Dismantled and shipped to Paris, today it is in the Frick Collection in New York.

All we see at first glance is a profusion of blues and pinks that tells a conventional love story in four episodes. There is a touch of the troubadour style in the laced bodices, Spanish collarettes, dainty poses and pretty faces: we are reminded of the theater, and more precisely of the graces of light opera. We must not, however, overlook the odd setting

The Fête at Saint-Cloud (detail), undated. Oil.

in which the scene is played—there are too many flowers, too much verdure. The tangled growth spreads in all directions, overflows, smothers the shrubbery; the roses clamber over the balustrades, throw out long blossom-studded shoots; an ordinary boxed orange tree disgorges a medley of sunlight and greenery. From the leafy branches a statue of Venus shoots out in a leap that stretches its shape to the point of ugliness: we are put in mind of the exaggerations of the Mannerists or, rather, of Troger or Maulbertsch. The park dissolves in a multitude of shadowy dells and secret nooks, belches huge vapory plumes towards the sky. A whiff of pantheism pervades the frivolous scene. Allowing for certain differences, we might be in Zola's "Paradou."

It may seem far-fetched to mention that other Southerner in this context. But if, instead, we name Saint-Lambert or Delille, we realize at once the superiority that marks Fragonard as a great Baroque poet. Where in all Europe, at that time, could one find his like? That same exaltation of nature led to the vogue for the English garden and later dictated the descriptions of Bernardin de Saint-Pierre. But Fragonard's voice was stronger and went deeper.

In these pictures the actors and their pleasant story might lead us astray. But in *The Fête at Saint-Cloud* the pretext has vanished. This large landscape, commissioned by the Duc de Penthièvre for his Paris mansion, by a lucky chance that seldom occurs in France, has always remained in the same place and today adorns the dining-room of the Governor of the Banque de France. The subject is simplicity itself: the fair held on the last three Sundays of September every year, when vendors and mountebanks filled the old park with their booths. The sober composition is carefully based on the golden number and firmly defined by a broad triangle of trees that opens on the vertical of the fountain. But it is an odd picture nonetheless. A desultory light distributes patches of brightness, divides our attention between two symmetrical motifs, and leaves a great hazy hole in the center of the canvas. The figures are dwarfed by the mighty trees of the park, even by the two slender birches in the foreground. Leafy branches, golden, ashy, bluish, ranging from

The Fête at Saint-Cloud, undated. Oil.

amber to emerald, in vast profusion soar towards the immense cloudy sky, or mingle with the plume of the towering waterspout. What is left of the subject? The flickering lights of the mountebanks' stands, and the vividly sketched little groups of spectators that have the stiff grace of Goya's rustic scenes. Only a few accents of blue, red and gold disengage them from the medley of light and greenery in which nature, at once friendly and grandiose, displays all her magic without denying humanity or troubling it.

When we consider the kermesses depicted by Rubens and the other Flemish painters Fragonard was acquainted with, we realize the important part nature plays in these works of his. When we consider the Romantics who were soon to set man face to face with a hostile or indifferent nature, we recognize that Fragonard spoke in the spirit of the eighteenth century. But he spoke with the voice of a lyric poet. Observe Pater's *Fair at Bezons* (Metropolitan Museum) with its heavy theatrical structures. Or listen to Diderot, for all his talent, describe the park at Marly. He too feels deeply the mixture of order and neglect and the grandeur of nature in a half-tamed state. "What a spot, my love! Innumerable yews lead up to arbors of greenery whose airy elegance defies

View of the Seacoast near Genoa, undated.
Brush and bistre wash on white paper.

The Fête at Rambouillet or The Isle of Love, *undated. Oil.*

The Fête at Rambouillet or The Isle of Love (detail), undated. Oil.

description. As they rise still higher, those arbors lead the eye to a woody background where the trees are only pruned directly above the arbors. The rest is rustic, bushy and wild. You should see the effect that makes!" The feeling is the same; so we appreciate all the more Fragonard's language.

His lyric vein had its source in Italy. In Rome and the Roman Campagna, which he roamed with Hubert Robert, this Southerner seems to have found the secret of a long-forgotten poetry. He saw nature in all her simplicity and is no less truthful in conjuring up the *Fontanone* at Tivoli (red chalk, Besançon Museum) than in drawing Bergeret's country seat at Nègrepelisse (*ditto*, Boymans-Van Beuningen Museum, Rotterdam) or sketching a picnic lunch (*ibidem*). On his travels he never stopped "gleaning," as Bergeret called it. But he was no less ready to transfigure what he saw. In *The Storm* (Louvre) he has transformed a pastoral episode into a drama. The rows of cypresses that reach up to the cloudy sky (Villa d'Este series, red chalk, Besançon Museum) and the

The Fête at Rambouillet or The Isle of Love (detail), undated. Oil.

copses in *The Little Park* (Wallace Collection) form thick arches that conceal the architecture. Hubert Robert multiplied allusions to antiquity, ruins, the contrasts between past and present. Fragonard dispensed with these effects. Was it because his sense of destiny was seldom tinged with melancholy? Or because he had not been educated in that classical tradition which makes a man so sensitive to the poetic overtones of the Italian landscape? Robert, it must be remembered, had studied at the Collège de Navarre and knew his Virgil. Fragonard, whose sensibilities had not been formed in the Latin Quarter, looked to nature alone. But he was capable of feeling nature to the point to exaltation.

The Fête at Rambouillet (Gulbenkian Foundation, Lisbon) shows how lofty is his poetry. The origin of the title, apparently of recent date, is uncertain. How can we possibly recognize, in this picture, the rural tranquillity of the manor and the peaceful banks of the vast pool? A barge loaded with musicians and pairs of lovers nears a leafy grotto close to a cascade. A gay throng presses against the balustrade—mere patches of purple and yellow set in a strange landscape. Roses spread a carpet right down to the water's edge. An uncanny light, neither midday nor evening, bathes a tousled vegetation, casts rainbow tints on distant statues, edges the bowers with sulphur. The cold colors, offset by a few touches of violet and yellow, culminate in deep blues, conjuring up a world of velvet and jewels. Out of this gorgeous setting rises the gaunt, gnarled silhouette of a tall tree; it recalls sixteenth-century German prints—Fragonard may have known them too—or, better still, the elaborate Chinese decorations that were in vogue at the time. But he may have merely transmogrified a motif which he took from the Dutch landscape painters and which occurs in many of his works. For the tree tossed there like a streak of lightning, half gold, half fire, is like the signature of the visionary. How far removed is this new voyage to Cythera from Watteau's melancholy pilgrimage. The characters have dissolved, their amorous sentiments, even their grace, have disappeared. What is left is a passionate music that carries off the shadowy lovers on the stream. It has a touch of Mozart, but already heralds Beethoven.

ROMANTIC PASSION

Historians are used to counting in centuries and start a new chapter in the evolution of art and thought whenever the century changes, without pausing to consider how arbitrary such divisions are. Thus Romanticism, in France at least, is held to be a nineteenth-century phenomenon and all its manifestations prior to 1800 are confidently described as premonitory signs of it. We must, however, admit that the need for effusion and escape which is the only acceptable definition of Romanticism had already found some of its major expressions in Young's *Night Thoughts*, Rousseau's *Nouvelle Héloïse*, Goethe's *Werther*, Bernardin de Saint-Pierre's *Paul et Virginie* and Fragonard's *Fête at Rambouillet*.

The situation is unfortunately confused by an ambiguity that was hardly felt at the time but makes a strong impression on us today. For that period witnessed the revival and rapid development of a taste for antiquity that we consider typically "classical." We find it impossible to believe that it was chiefly a response to the contemporary need for dreams and unreality. That André Chénier murmurs

> Alas! There flows in my uneasy soul
> A deep and silent melancholy...

The Kiss, undated. Bistre wash.

matters not at all. He speaks too often of Hyacinth and Clinias, of nymphs and nereids, for us to place his melancholy in the same class as Obermann's. The phenomenon is more obvious still in the visual arts. We cannot possibly bracket together Roman tunics and troubadours' hose, Brenet's *Death of du Guesclin* and David's *Andromache Weeping over Hector's Body*. We judge by hindsight and know that later those inspirations developed two quite different languages. The picturesqueness of knights in armor, moonlit trysts, battlements and burial vaults clashes with the heroic nude torsos borrowed from antique sculpture and the severe taste for architecture in the manner of Poussin. Ossian soon had his language; Homer and Livy theirs. But only after much confusion. The break became manifest when in David's own studio the sect of the "Primitives" was faced with the faction of the "Muscadins" (dandies), who harked back to a medieval, catholic past. The day arrived when David, before Girodet's *Victory Leading the Shades of French Warriors into Odin's Palace*, confessed to the painter: "I cannot understand that kind of painting. No, my good friend, I cannot understand it at all." It is easy to see that from then on antiquity became for French artists what it had been for the followers of Poussin, namely, an instrument of discipline. But for one or two generations it had chiefly represented a means of escape, perhaps the most attractive for an age that sought refuge from the tyrannical impact of social life and its factitious pleasures. Suffice it to mention the brief but amazing adventure of Maurice Quai and his friends, their youthful intransigence, their exaltation (not even outdone by the young Romantic writers grouped around Victor Hugo), the religious enthusiasm with which they preached a return to ancient Greece.

Consequently the grand Romantic transports are the outcome of an inspiration which was either antiquarian or more or less imbued with the lessons of antiquity. They were even expressed in a common language, whether in verses modeled on Virgil or Theocritus or in the precise drawings, which enclosed the volumes in an abstract outline, that young painters learned not only from Roman statues but also from the "Etrus-can" vases and the paintings by Raphael's predecessors that were beginning to attract attention. There is no great distance between Flaxman's drawings and Fuseli's, while Blake's visions merely transform David's nude figures into bloated puppets. David's teaching intervenes continually between Doyen's *St Genevieve* and Géricault's *Raft of the Méduse*. Yet the transition was quite natural from Baroque formulas to Romantic expression, from the stormy lyricism of Baroque inspiration to the violence and ostentation of Romantic passion. The stage we are accustomed to term Neoclassicism, which was so beneficial for all the arts, seems like a detour. This becomes quite clear when we consider the few great painters who bypassed it. In fact, Maulbertsch, in Austria, linked his exasperated visions and mysterious chiaroscuros to Tiepolo's example while, in Spain, Goya passed direct from the courtly painting of the eighteenth century to the solitary meditations of the Deaf Man's House.

Fragonard, though he hardly resembled those two artists, shared the same privilege. This is a clear mark of his originality. He proceeded direct from Boucher to the grand lyricism of the Romantics. No doubt, being sensitive to fashion, he did not entirely escape the taste of his day. How could his brush maintain all its impetuosity when, in 1773, he saw the king's mistress replace his canvases with Vien's and the pamphleteers hold up his "daubs" to public ridicule. His handling, as we have seen, became more taut, but his inspiration was not affected. This Parisian from the South could never take spear and chlamys seriously; grave citizens and the gods of Olympus were not in his line. *The Warrior's Dream* in the Louvre is so little in harmony with the new-fangled cult for the heroic that it is generally—though quite wrongly—believed to have been painted before 1765. Unlike Rousseau, who could unite the sentiment of *La Nouvelle Héloïse* with the dream of a society governed by virtue, or Chénier, who fired Greek myths with the most ardent passion, Fragonard was not attracted to the ancient world. He had no need to take refuge in history. It was from the themes dear to his youth that, imperceptibly as if by probing deep down in his soul, he achieved a new poetry.

The Besançon Museum has an admirable wash drawing heightened with watercolor which, for want of a better title, has been called *The Bed of State*. It is a bed—nothing more, nothing less—with ample festooned curtains; a bit too large, a bit too deep, smothered in clouds and cushions: obviously a dream bed. On looking closer we can spy swarms of little cupids frolicking gaily among its many folds; at its head, a pillow,

The Dream of Love or The Warrior's Dream, undated. Oil.

The Invocation to Love, undated. Oil.

a huge one. But the bed is empty: just to let us know that it is the bed desire dreams of. Here every detail is in Boucher's line. There is another drawing, in the Albertina, entitled *The Kiss*, in which Fragonard has repeated the same lozenge-shaped composition, the same effect of broad diagonals. But now it is night. And the bed is no longer smothered in lace, it is a broken sarcophagus under a spreading canopy of foliage. Amidst the cupids a winged genius brandishes a torch: but how different is the mood from *All Ablaze*! The torchlight rends the darkness revealing, in the center of the funereal couch, two bodies tightly embracing, two pairs of lips that seek each other, two souls. It was Horace who said "*Spirat adhuc Amor, vivunt commissi calores.*" Yet Lamartine and Musset were not more serious when they mingled the grand eternal themes of bed and tomb, death and love.

The full development of this inspiration can be traced in Fragonard's last works. Motifs dear to the literature of the day, which occur frequently in the Salons after 1775, acquire an unexpected resonance. The young woman carving an S on the trunk of a tree in *The Souvenir* (Wallace Collection) is Julie dreaming of Saint-Preux. Here Rousseau's sentiment is wrapped in a delicate poetry, with misty distances, blended contours, a subtle backlighting, and verdure in the manner of Corot, besides refinements of handling and a touch of the mundane that give the picture a curious affinity with those of the English portrait painters. *The Votive Offering to Love*, engraved by Mathieu, with its contemporary dress and grand theatrical gestures, has the same rather vulgar eloquence as the novels of that day. Symbols served Fragonard to attain the loftiest poetry. *The Sacrifice of the Rose* (private collection) has all the pertness of Parny's *Lendemain*:

> In your lovely eyes soft languor
> Follows shy reserve...

but Fragonard found a gravity and a passion that we might seek in vain in the witty, lively verses of Eleonora's lover. Yet there is nothing to match *The Fountain of Love* in the Wallace Collection or *The Invocation to Love* that we can admire in the precious little sketch in the Louvre.

The former borders on the ridiculous. The two athletic figures, striding side by side and refreshed at the winning post by a swarm of helpful cupids, derive from the most frigid tradition of allegorical painting. Yet we are blind to all but the sublime: an aspiration that comes from the depth of the soul, a thirst comparable to the yearning for infinity. *"Sicut cervus ad fontes aquarum..."*: a few minor alterations and this would be the fountain of divine love. The dark shadows, the monochrome coloring barely illuminated by a touch of ash green, the indistinct mingling of leaves and clouds, like the setting of a dream, the tense expression of the two faces depicted in severe profile at the very center of the canvas, even the invincible yet frozen impetus that recalls Zeno's runner: every detail tends to make the picture the symbol of an inner vision. Appealing, boldly, but by scarcely perceptible signals, to the spectator's most intimate experience.

The same chiaroscuro, which Fragonard took from Rembrandt and which transfigures the subject and clothes it in mystery, also occurs in *The Invocation to Love*. A shaft of pallid light falls on the rounded cheeks, brightened with a few touches of vermilion, of a young girl who might almost have escaped from a canvas by Rubens. But what is her strange dream? Here too there are neither smiling faces nor stagy gestures, but a sort of levitation that wafts away the body in an absolute dedication. Is it sensual pleasure or spiritual rapture? Or both at once? Who is that all-conquering Eros half hidden in the shadows? And what philter does he offer to lovers? There is no answer but the insistence on the mystery, as if that was the true nature of love. This lyricism, which exalts passion while shielding its mystery, gives us the measure of Fragonard's revulsion from the vision—clear even in disorder, quizzical even in pleasure or melancholy—which had been typical of the eighteenth century after Watteau and often was so still. It gives us the measure of the distance which the artist had traveled since *The Swing* and *The Orgy*.

It might be used as the foundation on which to build up a romantic Fragonard and thus efface the all too facile image of the Fragonard who painted the *Girl Dancing Her Dog on Her Bed*. But I have no such intention. After all, the same brush painted the *Girl Dancing Her Dog, The Lover Crowned* and *The Invocation to Love*. It is a mistake, if I may say so once again, to imprison Fragonard in a single formula. The eighteenth century offers many minor "masters of the boudoir" whose licentious works can vie with his, as proved by the quantity of trivia unduly attributed to him. Prud'hon too veiled his amorous transports in a mysterious penumbra. But when we find such different accents in the œuvre of a single painter we discover, beyond the peculiar poetry of each canvas, the unbroken line of his artistic creation and its inner significance.

The Fountain of Love, before 1785. Oil.

For behind this unceasing endeavor to depict love's every aspect there is more than the insouciance of a light-weight poet who changed his muse with every breeze. "The Cherubino of erotic painting," is what the Goncourts called Fragonard. But the comparison is mistaken if Cherubino was merely a feckless page who flitted greedily from flower to flower, always charming, always frivolous. Fragonard's art ranges from sensuality to passion. More than any of his fellow artists he was the painter of love. There are painters of woman, like Vouet and Ingres; painters of luscious flesh, like Rubens and Renoir; others have occasionally evoked love in charming pictures. But how many have dedicated their entire œuvre to scrutinizing love itself, its mysteries, and its many metamorphoses?

One, of course, was Watteau who discovered still more subtle shades. But their juxtaposition pinpoints Fragonard's privileged position. Watteau, like most other painters, sought to create a world of his own and all his life long was content to multiply images similar in their diversity. Creative artists of his type are easily recognized. All they do immediately enters a hermetically closed universe over which they hold sway and to whose unity their poetry owes its force. Fragonard was not one of them. The many pictures he painted do not constitute a coherent world. His brush and his spirit remain unchanged; but when we contemplate *The Swing* and *Now Say Please*, *The Fête at Rambouillet* and *The Fête at Saint-Cloud*, we miss the subtle common factor which gives a painter's œuvre its unity, and thanks to which—by way of example—Rubens's Andromedas and Didos belong to the same world as his Crucifixions. In Fragonard this is due neither to diffidence nor to impotence. It is typical of a spirit that dominated art and did not use it as a refuge. Each of his canvases gave him an opportunity to show man and nature in a new light, to explore their infinite possibilities, not to seek in them his own reflection. Few artists have worked in this way—a way that often baffles art lovers and detracts from his reputation. But, deep down, it holds a spiritual lesson. For unity passes from the creation to the creator, and an œuvre in its entirety denotes not an idea or an intuition but an attitude towards the world, not a fixed view of humanity or a challenge to fate but a quest that involves many vicissitudes and sometimes elicits a response.

Is this the paradox of *le bon Frago*? The painter who was long considered the most brilliant of improvisers attains the loftiest peaks of plastic language. The poet whose work was viewed as embodying the frivolity of his century lets us glimpse, beneath his lyric accents, a truly spiritual meditation.

Paris, September–December 1966.

BIOGRAPHY AND BACKGROUND

1732 April 6: Christening at Grasse (near Cannes) of Jean-Honoré Fragonard, first child of François Fragonard, "merchant," and of Françoise Petit, daughter of Louis-Joseph Petit, "merchant." The child is named after his grandfather, Jean-Honoré Fragonard, "merchant."

1732 Birth of Beaumarchais and Haydn.

1733 July 26: Christening of Joseph Fragonard, son of François Fragonard and brother of the future painter; the godfather is Joseph Gérard, a perfumer, whose daughter later became the painter's wife. The child died on May 23, 1734, and Jean-Honoré was left the only son.

1733 Birth of Hubert Robert.

1734 Birth of Restif de La Bretonne.

1737 Birth of Bernardin de Saint-Pierre.

1738 François Fragonard moves from Grasse to Paris with his family (if we are to believe the certificate of good citizenship issued to the painter in 1794, in which it is stated that he had been a resident of Paris for fifty-six years).

1738 Birth of Benjamin West and the Abbé Delille, future author of *Les Jardins*.

1740 Birth of the Marquis de Sade.

1741 Birth of Choderlos de Laclos and Chamfort.

1746-1752 Probable apprenticeship of the young Honoré first to a notary, then to Chardin, and finally to Boucher.

1746 Chardin exhibits at the Salon the replicas of his *Saying Grace* and *Recreations of Private Life*. Death of Largillierre. Birth of Goya.

1747 Publication of *Réflexions sur quelques causes de l'état présent de la peinture en France* (Reflections on Some Causes of the Present State of Painting in France) by La Font de Saint-Yenne. Death of Solimena and of G.M. Crespi.

1748 Birth of David.

1749 Departure for Italy of Madame de Pompadour's brother, the Marquis de Marigny, accompanied by Cochin. Death of Pierre Subleyras in Rome. Birth of Goethe.

1750 Boucher paints *Apollo and Issé* (Tours Museum).

1751 The Marquis de Marigny succeeds Lenormant de Tournehem as Surintendant des Bâti-ments (superintendent of royal buildings).
Publication of the *Encyclopédie* begins.

1752 Fragonard, competing for the Prix de Rome, wins first prize with his "Jeroboam Sacrificing to the Idols" (Ecole des Beaux-Arts, Paris).

Pierre Fragonard, priest and doctor of divinity, uncle of the young painter whom he named his heir in 1743, is buried in the Dominican Church at Grasse.

1752 Boucher obtains from Marigny the studio in the Louvre left vacant by the death of the court painter, Charles Antoine Coypel.
Publication of the first volume of *Recueil d'Antiquités égyptiennes, étrusques, grecques et romaines* (Collection of Egyptian, Etruscan, Greek and Roman Antiquities) by the Comte de Caylus.

1753 May 30: Fragonard enters the Ecole des Elèves Protégés, directed by Carle van Loo. While there he paints "Psyche Shows Her Sisters the Presents She Has Received from Cupid," exhibited at Versailles the following January (now lost).

1753 Birth of Parny and Rivarol.

1754 May 18: The Confraternity of the Blessed Sacrament at Grasse decides to commission a picture for their chapel from "Sieur Fragonard, of this town, resident of Paris." The young painter executes "Christ Washing the Feet of the Apostles," finished before April 1755 (still in Grasse Cathedral).

1754 La Font de Saint-Yenne publishes his *Sentiments sur quelques ouvrages du Salon de 1753* (Feelings about Some Works at the Salon of 1753). The Comte de Caylus reads his paper *Sur la peinture des Anciens* (On the Painting of the Ancients) before the Academy.

1755 Carle van Loo exhibits his *Spanish Conversation* (Hermitage, Leningrad) at the Salon.
Two pastels by Raphael Mengs, *Pleasure* and *Innocence*, brought to Paris by the Baron d'Holbach and greatly admired.
Winckelmann's *Gedanken über die Nachahmung der griechischen Werke in Malerei und Bild-hauerkunst* (Reflections on the Imitation of Greek Works in Painting and Sculpture) published in Dresden; a French version published in instalments in Fréron's *Journal étranger* in Paris starting the following January.
Birth of Elisabeth Vigée-Lebrun and of John Flaxman.
On November 1, 40,000 die in earthquake at Lisbon, causing a great stir throughout Europe and impassioned disputes on the notion of Providence.

1756 Fragonard leaves for Rome, arriving there in December.

1756 Birth of Mozart.

1756-1761 Fragonard in Rome as boarder at the French Academy, then under the direction of Natoire. There he is on intimate terms with Hubert Robert (in Italy since 1754) and meets Greuze (who arrives with the Abbé Gougenot in January 1757). He becomes the friend and protégé of the Abbé de Saint-Non who, arriving with Taraval in November 1759, takes him with him to work at Tivoli during the summer of 1760 and sends him to Naples early in 1761.

During this period Fragonard paints a "Study of a Man" and a "Head of a Priestess" (sent to the Academy in 1758) besides a large number of other studies (all lost); he copies Pietro da Cortona's "St Paul Restored to Sight" (1758, lost) and several landscapes, one of which is "The Storm" in the Louvre (drawing dated 1759).

1756-1763 The Seven-Year War.

1756 Natoire decorates the ceiling of San Luigi dei Francesi, Rome.

1757 Birth of Canova.

1758 Birth of Prud'hon.

1759 Deshays admitted to the Academy with his *Hector Exposed on the Bank of the Scamander* (Musée Fabre, Montpellier); Doyen accepted for his *Death of Virginia* (Pinacoteca, Parma).
Diderot begins his *Salons*.

1760 Death of G.A. Guardi. Benjamin West in Italy. Pompeo Batoni paints *The Downfall of Simon Magus* in Santa Maria degli Angeli, Rome. Maulbertsch decorates the ceiling of the library in the Barnabite monastery at Mistelbach, Austria.

1761 Fragonard accompanies the Abbé de Saint-Non back to France via Bologna, Venice, Piacenza and Genoa; the two friends are back in Paris at the end of September.

1761 Mengs executes *Parnassus* in the Villa Albani, Rome; Vien *The Corinthian Girl*; Greuze *The Village Betrothal*. Jean-Jacques Rousseau publishes *La Nouvelle Héloïse*.

1762 Date of Saint-Non's "Dancing Bear," an etching after Fragonard.

1762 Birth of André Chénier.

1763 Publication of four "Bacchanals" under the title "Set of Etchings Engraved in Italy by Fragonard."

1763 At the Salon Restout exhibits *Orpheus Descends to Hades* (Rennes Museum); Doyen *Ulysses and Andromache* (lost, but engraved); Vien *La Marchande d'Amours* (Palace of Fontainebleau).
Tiepolo is summoned to Spain.

1764 Fragonard engraves "The Little Park" and a set of etchings after Italian masters.

1764 Gavin Hamilton's *Andromache Weeping Over Hector's Body* and *Achilles Mourning for the Death of Patroclus*, made known by Cunego's engravings.
Saint-Lambert's *Les Saisons*.

1765 Fragonard submits his "Coresus and Callirrhoe" (Louvre, initial sketch in Angers Museum) to the Academy and is accepted unanimously. At Cochin's suggestion, Marigny buys the picture, commissions another to match, decides to have both works made into tapestries at the Gobelins, and gives Fragonard the studio in the Louvre left vacant by the death of Deshays.

Fragonard is present at the Salon for the first time, with his "Coresus," which receives great praise, a landscape "belonging to Bergeret de Grancourt" (?), "The Parents' Absence Turned to Account" (Hermitage) and two "Views of the Villa d'Este at Tivoli." Published in the same year is "Raccolta di vedute disegnate d'apresso natura..." (Collection of Views Drawn from Nature), a small folio containing six engravings by Saint-Non after Fragonard and Hubert Robert.

1765 Death of Carle van Loo.

1766 Fragonard's "The Lost Forfeit" (Metropolitan Museum, New York; sketch in the Hermitage, Leningrad) is engraved, probably in Rome, by Brachet (according to Louis Réau).

1766 Publication of Diderot's *Essai sur la Peinture* (Essay on Painting) and of a French translation of Winckelmann's *Geschichte der Kunst des Altertums* (History of Ancient Art), first published in 1764.
Houdon, in Rome, executes his *St Bruno* for Santa Maria degli Angeli. Benjamin West exhibits his *Pylades and Orestes* at Spring Gardens, London.

1767 At the Salon Fragonard exhibits "Groups of Children in the Sky, an oval picture" (lost?), a "Head of an Old Man, a circular picture" and several drawings. The critics, with Diderot at their head, express great disappointment.

The Baron de Saint-Julien, on Doyen's refusal, commissions from Fragonard the picture that became famous as "The Swing" (Wallace Collection, London). Saint-Non publishes the first of his sets of plates after Italian pictures engraved by the aquatint method from drawings by Fragonard.

1767 Doyen's *Miracle des Ardents* or *St Genevieve Putting an End to a Pestilence* (Paris, Church of Saint-Roch) exhibited at the Salon.

1768 September 21: Marriage contract between Jean-Honoré Fragonard, "painter to the King at his Royal Academy," and Marie-Anne Gérard, aged twenty-two.

1769 June 17: Jean-Honoré Fragonard and Marie-Anne Gérard married in the church of Saint-Lambert at Vaugirard, Paris.

December 10: Christening of their daughter Henriette-Rosalie Fragonard in the parish church of Saint-Eustache, Paris.

1769 Le Tourneur adapts Young's *Night Thoughts* in a French translation that has a huge success. Ducis stages a *Hamlet* after Shakespeare.

1770 June 24: Drouais sells Madame du Barry for 1,200 livres four overdoors painted by Fragonard and belonging to him; they are meant for the pavilion built for the king's mistress at Louveciennes (two now in the Louvre and Toulon Museum). Before the end of the year, Fragonard is apparently commissioned by Madame du Barry to decorate a drawing-room in the same pavilion; the execution of these panels (Frick Collection, New York) keeps him busy till the beginning of 1773.

December 10: On the recommendation of Pierre, who has succeeded Cochin as his adviser, Marigny asks Fragonard and Huet for four pictures for the king's dining-room at Versailles; Fragonard's were never executed.
Saint-Non marks this date on "The Farm" (or "The Restive Donkey"), an aquatint after a drawing by Fragonard (done probably when he was in Italy).

1770 Death of Boucher and Tiepolo. Birth of Thorvaldsen and Beethoven.

1772 The "Mercure de France" announces two prints by F. Godefroy after paintings by Fragonard: "Annette at the Age of Fifteen" and "Annette at the Age of Twenty."

1773 Fragonard quarrels with Mademoiselle Guimard, a famous dancer who had asked him to decorate her house; the paintings begun by Fragonard are completed by the young David.

At the Salon Vien exhibits "Two Greek Girls Crown Cupid with Wreaths" (Louvre) and "Two Greek Girls Take an Oath Never to Love" (Prefecture, Chambéry), the first of four panels for Louveciennes replacing those painted by Fragonard.

Publication of "Dialogues sur la peinture," an anonymous work attributed to Renou, which launches a brutal attack on Fragonard (among others), his pictures at Louveciennes, his style, and his friends.

1773-1774 Bergeret takes Fragonard and his wife with him to Italy; they leave Paris on October 4, pass through Limoges and Cahors, spend some time on Bergeret's estate at Nègrepelisse, and from there, travelling via Toulouse, Marseilles, Genoa and Florence, reach Rome on December 5. Except for a trip to Naples they stay in Rome until July 8 of the following year, when they leave for Paris via Bologna, Padua, Vienna, Dresden, and Frankfurt. On the journey, Fragonard does many drawings, some of which are still extant.

1773 Fuseli, in Rome since 1770, begins his *Macbeth* (drawing in Zurich, Kunsthaus).

1774 Death of Louis XV. Turgot introduces financial reforms and proclaims the free circulation of grain and flour. The Comte d'Angiviller becomes superintendent of royal buildings.

1775 Fragonard's sister-in-law, Marguerite Gérard, a girl of fourteen, joins the painter's family and becomes his pupil.

1775 Vien becomes head of the French Academy in Rome where David, who at last received the Rome Prize the year before, is accepted as a boarder. Abilgaard, in Rome since 1772, paints his *Philoctetes Wounded* (National Museum, Copenhagen).
Goya delivers his first cartoons to the Royal Tapestry Works at Madrid.
Publication of *Le Barbier de Séville* by Beaumarchais, *Le Paysan perverti* by Restif de La Bretonne, and *Les Idylles* by Léonard.

1776 Saint-Non publishes "The Sheepfold," an aquatint after a drawing by Fragonard (probably done during his stay in Italy).

1776 Guilds are suppressed in France, and statute labor abolished. Turgot is dismissed in May and Necker entrusted with financial administration.
Beginning of the American War of Independence.
Goethe's *Werther*, which met with great success when first published two years previously, is translated into French.

1777 The "Mercure de France" announces a print engraved by Delauny after Fragonard's "The Happy Family" and the publication by instalments of "Tableaux de la Suisse et de l'Italie," which includes "A Journey to Naples and Sicily," a monumental work edited by Saint-Non with illustrations by Fragonard and Hubert Robert (actually published between 1778 and 1786).
Saint-Non, still Fragonard's faithful friend, becomes an associate member of the Academy of Painting and Sculpture.

1777 Brenet paints *The Death of Du Guesclin* (Versailles Museum); Le Tourneur publishes a French version of Ossian.

1778 **Date marked on a set of prints by Fragonard: "The Wardrobe" "entirely by the hand of the author," "The Tax Farmers," "Young Woman Seated on a Chest," and "To the Genius of Franklin," engraved by Marguerite Gérard after Fragonard, and "The Swaddled Cat," also signed by her but probably engraved with assistance from her brother in-law.**

1778 Benjamin Franklin, on a mission to Paris, wins over the Court and the philosophers' party to the American cause and obtains French agreement to an alliance.
Death of Piranesi and Canaletto. Death of Voltaire and Rousseau.

1779 Death of Chardin and Mengs.

1780 **October 26: Christening at Grasse of Alexandre-Evariste Fragonard, the painter's second child, born on that day.**

Date marked on "The Elements Pay Homage to Nature" (disappeared since the Second World War).

1781 **March 4: François Fragonard, the painter's father, dies at Grasse.**

1781 Parny adds a Fourth Book ("Elegies") to his *Poésies érotiques*, the first version of which was published in 1778.

1782 **Fragonard and his wife buy "a house comprising two wings, with a forecourt, out-houses, a path to the river, near the Charenton quarries."**

1782 A memorial service for Poussin is held in the Pantheon, Rome. Fuseli exhibits *The Nightmare* in London with great success.
Delille publishes his *Jardins*, Laclos *Les Liaisons dangereuses*.

1783 **Date of print entitled "The Pre-arranged Flight," engraved by Macret and Couché after a painting by Fragonard.**

1784 **A print by Blot after "The Bolt" is advertised.**

1784 Beaumarchais's *Le Mariage de Figaro* is a huge success in Paris.

1785 **The "Mercure de France" announces a print by N.F. Regnault after Fragonard's "Fountain of Love." Death of Bergeret, succeeded at the Academy by Saint-Non as "honorary amateur member."**

1785 At the Salon David exhibits *The Oath of the Horatii*.

1787 **The "Mercure de France" announces several prints after Fragonard, "The Stolen Shift" by Guersant, "The Milk Jug" and "The Glass of Water" by Nicolas Ponce— proof that Fragonard's "frivolous" works are still popular.**

1787 Bernardin de Saint-Pierre publishes his novel *Paul et Virginie*.

1788 **October 8: Death of the artist's daughter Rosalie Fragonard, aged eighteen, at the Bergerets' country house at Cassan, near L'Isle-Adam.**

Publication of prints by Legrand after "My Shift is on Fire" and by Regnault after "The Stolen Kiss."

1789 September 7: Fragonard's wife and sister-in-law are members of the deputation of artists' wives who offer their jewelry to the National Assembly to pay off the public debt.

It is probably during this year that Fragonard, deeply affected by the death of his daughter, fell seriously ill.

1789 The Estates General meet (May 5) and revolutionary troubles begin.

1790-1791 The Fragonards, accompanied by Marguerite Gérard, leave Paris early in 1790 for Grasse where they stay with their cousin Alexandre Maubert until March 1791. The painter, having had the decorations painted twenty years before for Louveciennes sent on after him, arranges them in one of the rooms of the house and adds a number of panels to complete them.

Saint-Non publishes in 1790 his ''Recueil de griffonis'' which contains most of his engravings after drawings by Fragonard. He dies in Paris on November 25, 1791, soon after the painter and his family return from Grasse.

1790 Canova's *Cupid and Psyche* (Louvre).

1791 Volney's *Les Ruines, ou méditations sur les révolutions des empires*, an essay on the philosophy of history.

1792 Fragonard's twelve-year-old son Evariste is admitted to David's studio.

1792 The riots of August 10 initiate the violent phase of the French Revolution.

1793 Fragonard and his wife sell their house at Charenton. In December David proposes to the Convention to found a national Museum of Art and nominates Fragonard as particularly qualified for membership.

1793 The Terror (end 1793 to July 1794).
David's *Marat* (Brussels Museum).
Publication in Rome of Flaxman's illustrations to Homer.

1794-1800 Fragonard, appointed member of the Conservatoire of the Museum, is extremely active as President and Secretary (alternately), as attested by the archives. When the Museum is replaced in 1797 by the Central Museum of Arts, he is a member of the jury and supervises the transport of works of art from Paris to Versailles, where a special Museum of the French School had been set up.

He keeps the post until June 1800. The salary received during that period seems to have enabled his family to live through difficult times without too great hardship. In 1797 Fragonard, his wife and his sister-in-law pay 5,000 livres for a house at Evry-Petit-Bourg near Paris.

1794-1800 Reaction of Thermidor (July 1794); efforts at pacification and reorganization made by the Directoire (1795); the *coup d'Etat* of 18 Brumaire brings Bonaparte to power (1799); financial straits, devaluation of the *assignats*: annuities are now practically wiped out, reducing a great many people to destitution.

1796 In David's studio two groups of young artists come to the fore: the "Primitives" under Maurice Quai and the "Muscadins" inclined to religion and the Middle Ages.

1798 Goya paints the frescoes in San Antonio de la Florida, Madrid. Birth of Delacroix.

1799 Prud'hon exhibits *Wisdom and Truth Come Down to Earth* (Louvre) at the Salon.
David signs his *Rape of the Sabine Women* (Louvre).

1801 Gros paints his oil sketch of the *Battle of Nazareth* (Nantes Museum).

1802 Marguerite Gérard, Fragonard and his wife buy another house, in Paris this time, at 57, rue de l'Oursine (now rue Broca), for 12,000 francs.

1802 Chateaubriand publishes *Le Génie du Christianisme*.

1804 Marguerite Gérard is awarded a medal for her exhibit at the Salon.

1804 Chateaubriand's *René*.

1805 An imperial decree forces all artists to vacate their lodgings in the Louvre. Fragonard, who is granted a pension of 1,000 francs as compensation, takes rooms in the Palais-Royal district, in the house of Veri, a famous restaurant keeper.

1805 David painting *The Coronation of Napoleon*.
December 2: Napoleon victorious at Austerlitz.

1806 August 22: death certificate of "Jean-Honoré Fragonard, painter at the former Academy, aged 74 years 5 months, born at Grasse, died this day at five o'clock in the morning, Palais du Tribunat, house of Veri, restaurant keeper, district of the Butte des Moulins, husband of Marie Gérard. The witnesses were Messrs Alexandre-Evariste Fragonard, history painter, residing at 4, rue Verdelet, district of the Corn Market, son of the deceased, and Jean-Baptiste Alezard, landlord."

The death is commented on in various journals, which express praise of the painter —in particular the "Courrier des Spectacles" and the "Journal de Paris." On October 16, Le Carpentier reads a note on the painter before the Paris Society of Science, Letters and Arts.

Marie-Anne Fragonard went to live in the house at Evry-Petit-Bourg, where she died in 1824. Marguerite Gérard survived till 1837.

LIST OF ILLUSTRATIONS

SKIRA

TEXT AND COLOR PLATES PRINTED BY
IRL IMPRIMERIES RÉUNIES LAUSANNE S.A.

BINDING BY
H.+J. SCHUMACHER AG, SCHMITTEN (FRIBOURG)

PRINTED IN SWITZERLAND